D0898070

Victoria Kamhi and Joaquín Rodrigo on their wedding day in
Valencia, Spain, January 19, 1933.

A Singer's Guide to the Songs of Joaquín Rodrigo

Suzanne Rhodes Draayer

The Scarecrow Press, Inc.
Lanham, Maryland, and London
1999

SCARECROW PRESS, INC.

Published in the United States of America
by Scarecrow Press, Inc.
4720 Boston Way, Lanham, Maryland 20706
http://www.scarecrowpress.com

4 Pleydell Gardens, Folkestone
Kent CT20 2DN, England

British Library Cataloguing in Publication Information Available

Library of Congress Cataloging-in-Publication Data

Draayer, Suzanne Rhodes, 1952-
    A singer's guide to the songs of Joaquín Rodrigo / Suzanne Rhodes
Draayer.
        p.   cm.
    Includes bibliographical references and index.
    Discography: p.
    ISBN 0-8108-3676-9 (alk. paper)
    1. Rodgrio, Joaquín. Songs. 2. Songs--Analysis, appreciation. I. Rodrigo,
Joaquín. Songs. Texts. English & Spanish. II. Title.
ML410.R632D73   1999
782.42168'092--dc21   99-31780
                                                     CIP

⊖™ The paper used in this publication meets the minimum requirements of
American National Standard for Information Sciences—Permanence of
Paper for Printed Library Materials, ANSI/NISO Z39.48–1992.
Manufactured in the United States of America.

Contents

Foreword   vii
Preface   ix
Acknowledgments   xiii
Introduction   xv
1. The Composer's Biography   1
2. Victoria Kamhi and Her Life with Joaquín Rodrigo   13
3. *Canciones*   23
4. *Canciones de dos épocas*   91
5. *Cantos de amor y de guerra*   111
6. *Con Antonio Machado*   121
7. *Cuatre cançons en llengua catalana*   145
8. *Cuatro canciones sefardíes*   157
9. *Cuatro madrigales amatorios*   165
10. *Doce canciones españolas*   171
11. *Dos canciones para cantar a los niños*   191
12. *Dos poemas*   195
13. *La grotte*   205
14. *Líricas castellanas*   211
15. *Rosaliana*   217
16. *Triptico de Mosén Cinto*   231
17. *Villancicos*   243
Selected Discography   253
Video   255
Bibliography   257

General Index   261
Song Index   265
About the Author   267

Foreword

Dr. Suzanne Draayer has taken on a truly commendable task; that of creating a guide for Joaquín Rodrigo's vast catalogue of vocal works. Having for decades been a performer, a champion of and now in my later years, an avid teacher of Spanish and Hispanic vocal repertoire, I find this book of immense value, at it puts in perspective the body of vocal compositions of this most admired Spanish composer. The texts are carefully translated, and every line of text is transcribed phonetically in the IPA (International Phonetic Alphabet). I now feel that perhaps with the help of Dr. Draayer, I am not the only one, I am not the lonely Cid campeador, mounted on his steed, lance in hand, bringing knowledge of Spanish vocal music to the masses of singers who think of Spanish music as not much more than "Granada" and "La Cucaracha!"

Brava, Dr. Draayer! On with Albeniz, Granados, Turina, and De Falla!

With sincere admiration,

Nico Castel

Preface

The works of Joaquín Rodrigo have, unfortunately, been neglected in our music history texts, music appreciation texts, teaching studios, and many of our concerts. Some of this neglect is because of the difficulty in acquiring his music, and some is because of a bias toward Spain and Spanish musicians in general. One needs only to read *Grove's Dictionary of Music and Musicians* to discover that few Spanish composers are included. The works of those who are included are often regarded as inferior. In my study, I have found the same evaluations bandied from one resource to another, without foundation or substantiation. The purpose of this book is to advance Spanish music in general and the vocal music of Rodrigo in particular.

Lawrence B. Newcomb, a Rodrigo scholar states:

> Rodrigo is in no way a "one-hit" composer. He has given us over 250 works which, in the opinion of this writer, rival the *Concierto de Aranjuez* in their craftsmanship, expression of feeling, and sonic poetry. Similarly, the artist's originality must be firmly established. It is all too convenient to simply label him a "Spanish composer." The misconception that he is merely another musician dealing in Andalucian scales and dance rhythms inspired by flamenco singers, dancers and guitarists needs to be put to rest. The rich treasure chest of musical masterpieces by Rodrigo needs to be promoted. In this way, many more people can experience the enjoyment found in listening to and/or performing his

music. The artistic legacy of this twentieth century Spanish composer needs to be more clearly established and maintained.[1]

Joaquín Rodrigo is worthy of study, performance, and respect because of the quality of his compositions. Even as a very young man, he won many compositional awards in Spain, prizes that were awarded to only the most superior talents. Other awards were granted by France, universities in England and the United States, and other European countries and include the Order of Officier des Arts et Lettres (France), Coupe de la guitare (France), Member of the Société Européenne de la Culture, Member of the Académie Royale des Sciences, Des Lettres et des Beaux-Arts of Belgium, among others. I have not mentioned some of the prizes awarded by Rodrigo's native country--the Cervantes Prize, the Alfonso X el Sabio Fellowship, the National Music Award, and many others. These awards are not awarded capriciously, but are awarded to only the brightest and best.

Regarding his vocal music specifically, Rodrigo's choice of poetry proves him to be a man of great wisdom and learning. Languages include Ladino (the language of the Sephardic Jews), Castilian, German, French, Catalan, and Galician. The composer Franz Liszt set texts in five languages: Rodrigo surpasses even that record! Rodrigo set some of Spain's finest poetry, including works by Lope de Vega, Antonio Machado, San Juan de la Cruz, and others.

His compositional style also shows great variety and style. Some settings are in folk song style, with simple melodies, limited range, and easy piano accompaniments, as in *Doce canciones españolas*, written to represent some of the various regions of Spain. Other settings rank with those of Schubert and Schumann, utilizing intricate piano accompaniments, wide ranges, sensitive text settings, and lush, Romantic harmonies, as in *Con Antonio Machado*.

Rodrigo possesses the ability to appropriately set poetry from the Middle Ages through the twentieth century. In his *Cantos de amor y de guerra*, for example, all texts are ancient, but the first and fourth songs bear particular mention. The poetry of the first, "Paseábase el rey moro," dates from the ninth century. Because of its Arabic poetic style, Rodrigo used melodic ragas, rhythmic talas, and many melismas to imitate ancient Arabic song. The fourth song, "Sobre Baza estaba el rey," whose poetry dates from the eleventh century, is an exquisite setting, using very simple harmonies with a guitar-type accompaniment. The legend is beautifully and dramatically portrayed against this simple background.

Rodrigo, in his *Canciones de dos épocas*, performs the impossible! The first three poems date from the fourteenth and fifteenth centuries, whereas the last are the twentieth century poetry of Fina de Calderon. Additionally, the songs were composed six decades apart; the first three were composed in the late 1920s and the last two were composed in 1987, the final year Rodrigo composed. Yet the five create a composite group, beautiful to sing and exquisite to hear.

Finally, the songs are beautifully written for the voice. Phrases are expertly crafted, and melodies are sensuous and tuneful. The accompaniment never dominates the voice, but lovingly and masterfully supports it. Ranges are limited in the folk song-type pieces, but because many of the songs were composed for some of the world's finest singers--Teresa Berganza, Montserrat Caballé, Conchita Supervia, and others--some ranges, melodies, rhythms, and depth of poetry are demanding and challenging.

Finally, Rodrigo's music deserves to take its rightful place in the world. The Franco Regime, the Spanish Civil War, and the post- war era only served to isolate Spain's culture, musicians, and artists from the rest of the world. Because of this self-inflicted closed-door policy, the United States and the rest of the world have been unable to enjoy Spain's rich cultural heritage. Our song collections, concerts, printed music, music appreciation texts, and music history books have almost completely neglected the works of Spanish composers. It is hoped that change is in the near future.

Maestro Rodrigo's songs are now accessible to every singer and teacher. His vast song literature has been transcribed into International Phonetic Alphabet (IPA), and this book includes literal translations as well as idiomatic translations. Other details given are background information, range, length, and other relevant facts. Because of the diverse pronunciations and dialects of the Castilian language, the Nico Castel book, *A Singer's Manual of Spanish Lyric Diction*, has been used exclusively in the transcription of Castilian and Ladino texts into International Phonetic Alphabet. This valuable book should be in every singer's library. Other sources are cited in the bibliography.

A Singer's Guide to the Songs of Joaquín Rodrigo will acquaint you with some of the world's most beautiful vocal literature. Use it with your students and in your own recitals. You and your audiences will appreciate its profound beauty, inspiration, and charm.

Notes

1. Larry Newcomb, "Joaquín Rodrigo and Spanish Nationalism," University of Florida Master's Thesis. (1995), 7-8.

Acknowledgments

There are many people to whom I am indebted for their enthusiastic help and support of this project. Stephanie Leigh Vague, former assistant professor of Spanish at Winona State University (1996-1998), translated all the Castilian poems into English. This book would not have been possible without her assistance and review of my rough word-for-word translations. Stephanie holds a B.A. in Spanish and an M.A. in Hispanic Literature from the University of Minnesota. She is currently pursuing her Ph.D. in Hispanic Literature at the University of Iowa. Catalan texts were translated by Lucía Osa-Melero, a native of Cullera in the province of Valencia. Lucía, after study at the University of Valencia and the Mercator School of Translation and Interpretation in Ghent, Belgium, is now pursuing an M.A. in Education and Didactics at the University of Iowa. Carlos Laredo Verdejo, of Madrid, recorded Rosalía de Castro's five poems on audiotape so that I could transcribe them into IPA. Robert Hungerford, professor emeritus of Winona State University, edited and improved upon my French translations. Bob, after completing two degrees at the Julliard School of Music, spent many years studying, living, and performing in Paris.

Cecilia Rodrigo, daughter of Joaquín Rodrigo and agent and publisher of Ediciones Joaquín Rodrigo, graciously answered all my e-mail questions and spent hours of her time allowing me to interview her. The days I spent in her office in Madrid will be treasured and remembered for the rest of my life. Kathy Zegarra, also of Ediciones Joaquín Rodrigo, translated the Galician texts, articles, and lectures of Maestro Rodrigo, and like Cecilia, was a valuable part of the research process.

Carlos Laredo Verdejo, of Madrid, audiotaped the Galician poems so that I could transcribe them into International Phonetic Alphabet.

I must also thank Winona State University for their support of this project. A Professional Improvement Grant helped fund my research and travel to Spain. Roy Smith and Mark Erickson, research librarians at Winona State, frequently came to my aid and were always enthusiastic about helping me.

And finally, I must thank Professor George Shirley, whose vocal literature class at the University of Maryland inspired me to look beyond traditional literature to discover a wealth of neglected treasures in song.

Introduction

Do we as performers, musicologists, and music educators need a new paradigm? In recent years, we as a human race have attempted to think more globally in many arenas--politically, medically, economically, socially, environmentally, and so on. Our traditional music history books, music appreciation books, our performance repertoire, and the repertoire we teach in our studios must also be challenged. As Arden Hopkin, my colleague at Brigham Young University, said, "We have looked to western Europe too long." I must agree. The music of Germany, Italy, and France has dominated our teaching for decades. And these three countries do not constitute all of western Europe! The traditional paradigm must be reevaluated, as it has begun to be redefined regarding the work of women composers and musicians. Because ethnomusicology has challenged us to look beyond "cultivated" music and into the rich folk music heritage, we must develop a broader view of the world's music. Taking a look at our music appreciation and music history books, we would not suspect that there are composers living and working in Australia, Venezuela, Finland, or Portugal.

This book is an attempt to remedy a tiny facet of the problem. Spanish music, too, has been neglected. We are more likely to know the exotic imitations of Spanish music--Georges Bizet's *Carmen*, Giacchino Rossini's *Barber of Seville*, Claude Debussy's *Iberia*, and others, rather than the true rhythms, dances, melodies, and culture that inspired those simulations. The purpose of *A Singer's Guide to the Songs of Joaquín Rodrigo* is to permit the industrious singer and teacher to have an accessible guide to the poetry, translations, and pronunciations of Rodrigo's lovely songs, many of which are stepped in Spanish legends and history. With this guide, it is my aim that we as teachers and performers will broaden our cultural horizons and look beyond the traditional paradigm to discover a wealth of untapped music.

In our music history and appreciation texts, we study those composers who made huge contributions in the field and who influenced many composer following them. As a result, particularly in the twentieth century, we ignore completely those composers who did not advance atonal, musique concrete, electronic, aleatoric, or serial compositional style to a new height. Yet our audiences are generally more conservative, preferring lovely melodies, haunting rhythms, and understandable forms. Isn't it possible that there is a place for all types of music--the dissonant, highly innovative, modernistic style as well as the neo-Romantic, neo-Baroque, and neo-Classical?

Joaquín Rodrigo is a neo-Classical composer, favoring ancient legends as well as modern poetry, set in traditional art song style. At no time is the singer struggling to be heard over a massive accompaniment, because accompaniments are generally thin in texture. Rodrigo is a masterful melodist, creating exquisite themes that enhance the poem, and suit the singer's voice. He uses ancient Moorish melodies, Spanish folk rhythms, and dances in his accompaniments and melodies. His music is intensely nationalistic, professing a deep love and commitment to his homeland just as Aaron Copland, Leonard Bernstein, George Gershwin, and others have created idioms that are distinctly American.

Joaquín Rodrigo has not revolutionized music with new sounds or innovative compositional styles. Unlike those of Manuel de Falla and Enrique Obradors, his songs are not modern versions of folk songs, except for the ever popular *Cuatro madrigales amatorios*. Nor does he, like Joaquín Turina, rely on the cante jondo, guitar techniques, and vocalized, melismatic "ahs" in his songs. Rodrigo's songs meld the old with the new--supreme lyricism, harmonic as well as nonharmonic dissonance, and a fine sense of poetic line. Rodrigo and Victoria Kamhi, his wife, love languages, literature, and history, as is evident in his broad choice of poetry. Rodrigo has given Spain and the rest of the world a gift to be cherished--the history of Spain in song.

The Composer's Biography

Joaquín Rodrigo composed more than one hundred seventy works between 1923 and 1989. He composed prolifically for voice, guitar, orchestra, choir, piano, and other instruments, and in many genres. His music uniquely merges the ancient with neo-Classical elements, Romanticism with wit, humor, dissonance, and a profound respect for beauty of phrase and harmony.

He has set the most sublime poetry to music, and traversed Spanish musical geography with an inspiration which goes beyond the mere craft of composition. His honors, from many countries, the recognition of his qualities as a human being, as an academic, and as a professional musician, with awards, honorary degrees, and the membership of academies, societies and organizations of the greatest prestige, complete the profile of a remarkable human being, gifted with a great capacity for work, a refined sensibility, and abundant inspiration.[1]

The great maestro Joaquín Rodrigo was born in Sagunto, near Valencia, on November 22, 1901 (St. Cecilia's day). He was one of ten children, with three brothers and six sisters. Vicente Rodrigo Peirats, his father, was a merchant, and his mother, Juana Vidre Ribelles, although she had little formal education, appreciated the arts. As a result of a diphtheria epidemic, Rodrigo was blinded at the

1

age of three. The family home in Sagunto was near a rehearsal hall, the *Lyra Saguntina,* and Rodrigo would spend hours as a young boy listening to rehearsals and concerts. In 1906, the family moved about thirty miles away to the city of Valencia, where Rodrigo began studying music, first with Eduardo López Chávarri, the well-known composer, folklorist, and writer at the Conservatorio de Valencia. Later, he studied composition and harmony with Professor Francisco Antich. Rodrigo became an excellent pianist and a good violinist. Beginning in 1920, Rodrigo traveled throughout Europe for a number of years. In 1923, he composed his first important work, *Juglares,* which was soon premiered by the Valencia Orchestra. Two years later, his *Cinco piezas infantiles* for orchestra was awarded the National Prize.

In 1927, Rodrigo went to Paris and began a five-year study in composition with Paul Dukas at the Ecole Normale de Musique. Rodrigo's impression of that first meeting is all the more fascinating, considering his blindness:

> In 1927, in spite of my father's firm opposition, I traveled to Paris to complete my music studies. My dream, at that time, was to study with Ravel, but he did not teach classes.
>
> I was still somewhat undecided, when on one of those rainy November days, the Opera Comique presented Paul Dukas' opera, *Ariadna and Blue Beard.* I was an enthusiastic admirer of Dukas' glowing symphonic poem, "The Sorcerer's Apprentice" and I rushed off to that charming small theater which I had not yet visited. I emerged in a state of wonder and firmly determined to work with Dukas, if he would accept me as a student.
>
> At that time, I had met the hispanist, Henri Collet, and he gave me a letter of introduction to Dukas, professor of composition at the Conservatoire and at the Ecole Normale de Musique.
>
> How excited I was as I was approaching his house there in Passy, not far from the Bois de Boulogne. I recall that as I was inquiring of the concierge about the maestro, a rather short man with a big umbrella, which he always held onto, muffled in a thick beard, who was leaving the building responded, "I'm the one you are looking for." With great nervousness, I explained my purpose as well as I could in my meager French and I seemed to understand that he was asking me to go upstairs with him for a moment.
>
> The old building, the typical winding staircase, the very simple apartment, the small room where he worked with an old piano, a few mats, a chimney which didn't give much heat, and many, many scores and a great number of books. At that

moment, I became familiar with his French, spoken through his beard in an obscured voice, almost harsh voice. It appeared to me that he was trying to tell me to come to see him at the Ecole Normale de Musique and to bring some of my work. So I did. Paul Dukas was a rather distant person, very austere in his praise but just in his judgment, biting, yet far from sarcasms. He had that very affectionate something, that quality that emanates from the artist with dignity and he had made of his ideal a search for the truth and authenticity.

The lecture hall was spacious, this time with a grand piano and the Maestro seated before it, encircled by several known composers, among them Roland Manuel and the Mexican composer, Manuel Ponce, with whom I struck up a very solid friendship. In addition, there was a small group of students and pianists, almost all foreign. I happily passed the fearful test and months later, I can say without false modesty, I was his favorite student. Thanks to his intervention, much to my great surprise, I was able to publish a good number of my works. I remember that he said to me, "Rodrigo, when you go to see a publisher, don't forget that by no means are editors easy to entice." The following year, and again with his intercession, I was able to achieve the premiere of my first symphonic work, *Cinco Piezas Infantiles* by the Straram Orchestra, the most prestigious orchestra in Paris at the time.

I spent five courses as his student. Later, my wife, of whom the Maestro was very fond, and I continued with him as audit students until 1935, the year he died as a result of a heart attack, just after turning seventy. I recall a few weeks prior, he experienced the first serious attack. When I called him, inquiring how he was, he replied, "You can be at ease, it isn't my time." Unfortunately, the next time was.

The classes met twice a week and lasted two hours, divided in two parts: the first hour was for correcting works. The second hour, for me the most interesting, was analysis. Sitting at the piano, with me always at his side, Dukas would read symphonic works, chamber works, operas, etc. His judgment was always rapid, precise, showing great understanding and enormous scholarship. He was familiar with all kinds of music and his opinions were profoundly fair.[2]

Dukas said of Rodrigo: "I have seen the arrival in Paris of Falla, Albéniz, Rodrigo. I'm not sure that this last is not the most gifted of the three."[3]

Dukas's prophecy was proven to be true almost immediately. A review of the premier of *Cinco piezas infantiles* appeared in the French newspaper *Comaedia* on May 5, 1930. The critic, Louis Aubert, wrote:

Between Jacques Ibert's *Escales* and *La Mer* by Debussy, we were introduced to a young Spanish composer whose name, Joaquín Rodrigo, we will indeed remember. His *Cinq Pieces Enfantines* were charming and full of good humor, simplicity and sharp observation. They will take an honorable place in the line of music literature whose composers, starting with Schumann, have studied the heart and soul of children, their games and the awakening of their senses, culminating in Bizet and Moussorgsky.

These totally unpretentious pieces by Mr. Rodrigo are as graceful and naive as their title requires, given the circumstances that the composer is blind and has surmounted all of the obstacles inherent to his physical limitations and inherent to writing an orchestral score, it is evident that he has accomplished a "tour de force." His treatment of the orchestra, pleasant to listen to and free of conventional resources, is proof of a mastery which would be the envy of many who are blessed with sight. It is difficult to remember when we have encountered such assuredness and such ease in a young composer.[4]

Rodrigo always cherished this review because it was the first international recognition of his talent. He was only twenty-eight years old at the time. [5]

While in Paris, Rodrigo frequently kept the company of Manuel de Falla and other Spaniards living in Paris. Falla encouraged Rodrigo to compose nationalistic music that would employ Spanish dance rhythms, gypsy and Moorish melodies, and the accompanimental effects of the guitar.[6] When Falla was made a member of the "Légion d'Honneur," Falla invited Rodrigo to play some of his works on the prestigious concert held at the Rothschild Palace. Because of that concert, Rodrigo was awarded publishing contracts with Eschig Publishers and with Rouart & Lerolle.

In 1933, Rodrigo married the Turkish pianist Victoria Kamhi, and returned to Spain with her the following year. On receiving the Conde de Cartagena Grant, Rodrigo continued his studies with André Pirro at the Sorbonne and with Maurice Emmanuel at the Paris Conservatoire.

One may wonder why Joaquín Rodrigo, Joaquín Turina, Manuel de Falla, Isaac Albéniz, Enrique Granados, and other Spanish composers were drawn to Paris for musical study. The Spanish, as well as other foreigners studying in Paris, did not lose their individuality and national idioms, but were encouraged to utilize their nationalistic traits--ancient scales, dance rhythms, and musical forms. This speaks well of the French teaching methods and their inclusiveness.

Rodrigo escaped the immediate effects of the Spanish Civil War (1936-1939) by living in Paris and Germany. While in Paris, he completed his *Cuatro piezas para piano* and orchestral arrangements of Isaac Albéniz's *Sevilla* and de Falla's *Fire Dance*. He was also commissioned to compose the music for a movie on the life of Christopher Columbus. His song, "La Canción del grumete," was composed for that movie and was enormously popular with Spanish singers. At the war's conclusion, he happily returned to Madrid. His *Concierto de Aranjuez* premiered in 1940 with the Barcelona Philharmonic Orchestra, César Mendoza Lassalle, conductor, and Regino Sáinz de la Maza, guitarist. The work and its composer received an enthusiastic ovation in Barcelona and a few days later in Bilbao.

In 1942, Rodrigo composed his concerto for piano and orchestra entitled *Concierto heroico*. He entered this work, dedicated to his native city of Sagunto, in the National Award for Music competition and won. It premiered on April 6, 1943, with Leopoldo Querol, pianist, and Ernesto Halffter, conductor, in Lisbon with the National Orchestra. A few months later, his *Zarabanda lejana y villancico* was performed by the Berlin Chamber Orchestra. Other works of this decade include the *Concierto de estío* for orchestra and violin, the *Capriccio* for violin solo, *Cuatro madrigales amatorios*, for voice and piano, as well as its voice and orchestra score, and finally, his *Ausencias de Dulcinea*, a symphonic poem for orchestra, bass soloist, and four sopranos.

Rodrigo emerged as the leading postwar Spanish composer, and as a consequence of his prestige, he was appointed professor of music history at the University of Madrid. The Manuel de Falla Chair was created there for him in 1947, a position he held until 1978. Rodrigo was extremely prominent throughout sixty years of Spanish music although he did not create a school of followers. Indeed, the next generations of Spanish composers were more attracted by the new currents of dodecaphonic, aleatoric, and atonal music.[7]

Maestro Rodrigo's prizes, honors, and awards are numerous. For *Ausencias de Dulcinea*, he was awarded the Cervantes Grand Prize, and in 1950, he was elected to the Royal Academy of Fine Arts. Other commendations include the Cross of Alfonso X the Wise (1953), honorary doctorates from the University of Salamanca (1963), the University of Southern California (1982), the Polytechnic University of Valencia (1988), the University of Alicante (1989), the Universidad Complutense de Madrid (1989), and the University of Exeter (1990). In 1982, Rodrigo was awarded the Spanish National Award for Music. Additionally, he was awarded the Cross of the Legion d'honneur (1963), and in 1979, Rodrigo was elected to the

Royal Academy of Sciences, Letters and Fine Arts of Belgium, filling
the vacancy left by the death of Benjamin Britten. In 1991, the
Conservatory of Valencia was renamed in honor of Joaquín Rodrigo.

Cecilia Rodrigo writes:

> Rodrigo was raised to nobility in 1991 on his ninetieth birth-
> day, by H. M. Juan Carlos I, King of Spain, with the title
> "Marqués de los jardines de Aranjuez." In 1996, he was
> honored with Spain's greatest international distinction, the
> Prince of Asturias prize for the Arts, awarded to a composer for
> the first time. The following year, that prize was shared by
> Yehudi Menuhin and Mstislav Rostropovich.[8]

Rodrigo wrote numerous works for the piano, including *Suite*
(1928), *Preludio al gallo mañanero* (1926), and *Cinco sonatas de
Castilla con tocatta a modo de pregón* (1951). His most important
symphonic poem is *Per la Flor Lliri Blau* (1934) and other
important symphonic works include the *Concierto en modo galante*
(1949), *Concierto serenata* for harp and orchestra (1952), and
Fantasia para un gentilhombre (1954). One must also mention
Rodrigo's ballet, *Pavana real,* his zarzuela, *El Hijo Fingido,* his
opera, *La Azucena de Quito,* and his numerous songs for chorus.

There have been numerous "Rodrigo Festivals" organized around
the world, including Puerto Rico, London, Pittsburgh, Pennsylvania,
Turkey, Japan (Tokyo, Nagoya, and Osaka), and Mexico City.

Of his music, Rodrigo says:

> I don't think I would have been a musician if I had not been
> blind. I love history, and had I been able to read I think I
> would have become a professor of history, a poet or a phi-
> losopher.
>   I try to capture the spirit of the 16th, 17th, and 18th centuries
> in Spain and put it to music--not traditional Spanish music, but I
> modernize and intellectualize it.[9]
>   I learnt a great deal from Dukas, but studying under him I
> became even more Spanish than I was before. Indeed, I feel that
> composers today must keep to their national idioms. So much of
> modern music is monotonous because all the very young com-
> posers will write in the same atonal style.[10]

Rodrigo went on to say in an interview with a reporter from the
London *Times,* that he had learned much from Manuel de Falla.
Rodrigo, like Falla, used many regional melodies in his music but he
is also attracted to the musical traditions of Old Castile. Rodrigo

said:

> Valencia had very close relations with Castile, and I have always
> felt a close affinity with the spirit of this noble part of Spain.
> Indeed, one of my favorites among my own compositions is
> *Ausencias de Dulcinea*, which is scored for full orchestra, a bass
> voice and four sopranos.[11]

In a later interview regarding this work, Cecilia Rodrigo stated: "The
words are by Cervantes and it is important to my father to set music
to the literature of Spain. By bringing this poetry into contemporary
music he is a link between the past and the present."[12] This
philosophy is evident as one studies the Maestro's works. From his
instrumental works to his piano compositions, choral pieces and solo
songs, the past is beautifully intertwined with the present. The
history of Spain is cultivated and taught through text, harmonies and
instrumentation.

Rodrigo is well known as a song composer. Performers and audiences frequently enjoy his *Cuatro madrigales amatorios*, but he has
composed nearly one hundred songs, many of which are relatively
unknown in this country. Rodrigo, as a pianist, accompanied many of
Spain's finest singers and knows the voice and its capabilities well,
as is evidenced in his song literature. Cecilia Rodrigo writes:

> The true essence of his music is found in his vocal music and that
> his personality is reflected in the refinement and profound
> sensitivity of his sublime melodies, gift of an inspiration that few
> twentieth century composers can equal.[13]

Rodrigo considers the voice to be the perfect instrument, and his
most favorite is the soprano voice.

> As a lover of literature, I have always tried to combine my musical
> inspiration with some of the great poetic texts of Spanish
> literature. From my early youth, I wrote songs, the first one dating
> from 1925. My last compositions are also for the soprano voice
> and piano, dating from 1987. I have been acquainted with many
> great international singers, such as Victoria de los Angeles,
> Montserrat Caballé, Teresa Berganza, Pilar Lorengar and many
> others. Victoria de los Angeles premiered some of my songs. I
> personally provided the piano accompaniment for many sopranos
> who performed my songs in numerous concerts and have made
> many tours with sopranos to perform not only my
> works but those of other composers. [14]

Because some of his songs are bit low for a high soprano, I asked Maestro Rodrigo if he objected to transposition. I personally transposed *Doce canciones* and *Tres villancicos* in order to better fit my tessitura and range. He responded:

> I do not object to transposition if this brings them into the reach of a greater number of singers. However, most of my songs have been composed for a specific soprano voice, keeping in mind the particular range and qualities or characteristics of that voice.[15]

I also discussed with Maestro Rodrigo and Cecilia, his daughter, a-gent, and publisher of Ediciones Joaquín Rodrigo, the difficulty of acquiring Spanish music. Those who wish to order Rodrigo works may contact Ediciones Joaquín Rodrigo directly at their website, www.joaquin-rodrigo.com or email:ediciones@joaquin-rodrigo.com. Classical Vocal Repertoire, Glendower Jones, editor, maintains a huge inventory of Spanish vocal music and may be contacted at 1-800-298-7474 or e-mail: ClasVocRep@aol.com. The address is: 3253 Cambridge Avenue, Riverdale, NY 10463. Fax: 718-601-1969. The website at Classical Vocal Repertoire lists only four percent of their inventory.

A complete list of Rodrigo's solo vocal works is given below. A key to the symbols is on pages 11.

Aranjuez, ma pensee (1988)	lv, gtr	EJR
En Aranjuez con tu amor (1968)	lv, pf	EJR
Barcarola (1934)	mv, pf	Sch
Canción del cucu (1937)	lv, pf	Sch
Canción del grumete (1939)	mv, pf	Sch
Canciones de dos épocas	hv, pf	EJR-Sch
Cantiga (1925)		
Romance de la infantina de Francia (1928)		
Serranilla (1928)		
Árbol (1987)		
¿Por qué te llamaré? (1987)		
Cántico de la esposa (1934)	mv, pf or orch	EJR, Sch
Cantos de amor y de guerra (1969)	hv, pf or orch	EJR, UME
Paseábase el rey moro		
¡A las armas, moriscotes!		
¡Ay, luna que reluces!		
Sobre Baza estaba el rey		
Pastoricico, tú que has vuelto		
La Chanson de ma vie (1939)	lv, pf	EJR
Chimères (1939)	mv, pf	EJR

Con Antonio Machado (1970)   mhv, pf   EJR, UME
Preludio
Mi corazón te aguarda
Tu voz y tu mano
Mañana de abril
Los sueños
Cantaban los niños
¿Recuerdas?
Fiesta en el prado
Abril galán
Canción del Duero
Coplas del pastor enamorado (1935)   lv, pf   Sch
Cuatre cançons en llengua catalana (1935)
                                               hv, pf or orch   Sch
Cançó del Teuladí
Canticel
L'Inquietut Primaveral de la Donzella
Brollador Gentil
Cuatro madrigales amatorios (1947)
                                               lv or hv, pf or orch   Ch
¿Con qué la lavaré?
Vos me matásteis
¿De dónde venís, amore?
De los álamos vengo, madre
Cuatro canciones sefardíes (1965)   mv, pf   EJR
I. Respóndemos
II. Una pastora yo amí
III. Nani, nani
IV. "Morena" me llaman
Doce canciones españolas (1951)   mv, pf   Sch
1. ¡Viva la novia y el novio!
2. De ronda
3. Una Palomita blanca
4. Canción de baile con pandero
5. Porque toco el pandero
6. Tararán
7. En las montañas de Asturias
8. Estando yo en mi majada
9. Adela
10. En Jerez de la Frontera
11. San José y Maria
12. Canción de cuna
Dos canciones para cantar a los niños (1973)   mv, pf   EJR-UME
Corderito blanco
Quedito
Dos Poemas (1959)   mv, fl or pf   EJR-UME
Verde verderol
Pájaro del agua

10   Chapter 1

La espera (1952	hv, pf or orch	Sch
Esta Niña se lleva la flor (1934)	hv, pf	Sch
Estribillo (1934)	hv, pf	EJR, Sch
Folias Canarias (1958)	mv, pf or gtr	Sch
Fino cristal (1935)	mv, pf	Sch
La grotte (1962)	mv, pf	EJR
Líricas castellanas (1980)	hv, fl, oboe, gtr, or vih	Sch
Por mayo, era por mayo (Romancillo) (1950)		
	hv, pf	EJR, Sch, UME
Primavera (1950)	hv, fl, & pf	EJR
Romance de Comendador de Ocana (1948)		
	hv, pf or orch	EJR, UME
Romance de Durandarte (1955)	mv, gtr	EJR, UME
Rosaliana (1965)	hv, pf or orch	Sch
1. Cantart'ei, Galicia		
2. ¿Por qué?		
3. Adiós ríos, adiós fontes		
4. ¡Vamos bebendo!		
Sobre el cupey (1965)	mv, pf	Sch
Soneto (1934)	hv, pf	EJR, Sch
Tres villancicos (1952)	mhv, pf or gtr	Sch
Pastorcito santo		
Aire y donaire		
Coplillas de Belén		
Triptic de Mosén Cinto (1946)	hv, pf or orch	EJR-Sch
L'harpa sagrada		
Lo violí de Sant Francesch		
Sant Francesch y la cigala		

The new Rodrigo collection published by Schott--*Joaquín Rodrigo. 35 Songs for Voice and Piano*–is an excellent value and provides a variety of styles, poetry, and difficulty levels. This collection, expertly reviewed by Judith Carman in the *Journal of Singing*, (May/June 1997, page 61) makes a wonderful addition to any music library!

35 Songs for Voice and Piano	hv & mv, pf	EAM-Sch

This collection includes the following songs and song cycles:
   Doce canciones españolas canciones (1951)
   Barcarola (1934)
   Canticel (1935) (#2 in Quatre cançons en llengua catalana)
   Cántico de la esposa (1934)
   Canción del cucú (1937)
   Canción del grumete (1939)
   Canço del Teuladi (1934)
        (#1 in Quatre cançons en llengua catalana)
   Coplas del pastor enamorado (1935)

Esta Niña se lleva la flor (1934)
Estribillo (1934)
Fino cristal (1935)
Romancillo (Por mayo, era por mayo) (1950)
Sobre el cupey (1965)
Soneto (1934)
¡Un Home, San Antonio! (1950)
Cuatro canciones sefardíes (1965)
Tres villancicos (1952)
Two Arias from El Hijo Finjido ("The Impostor Son") (1963)
    Yo pagaré la posada
    Madre, un caballero

Key to Symbols:

Ch	J&W Chester Ltd.
EAM	European American Music
EJR	Ediciones Joaquín Rodrigo
fl	flute
gtr	guitar
hv	high voice
lv	low voice
mhv	medium high voice
mlv	medium low voice
mv	medium voice
orch	orchestra
pf	piano
Sch	Schott
UME	Unión Musical Española
vih	vihuela

Joaquín Rodrigo died of natural causes on July 6, 1999, at his home in Madrid. The world laments his loss as one of the most important Spanish composers of all time and as one of the most distinguished artists of the twentieth century. He will be remembered as a sensitive, humble man who portrayed the beauty of the Spanish countryside, its vibrancy and color, and its exquisite poetry, through passionate themes and rhythms. Although his ultimate and definitive silence leaves a void, preparations have already begun to celebrate the one hundredth anniversary of his birth in the year 2001.

Notes

1. Eduardo Bautista García, *Joaquín Rodrigo: A Compilation of Articles for the 90th Anniversary,* trans. Elizabeth Matthews and

Raymond Calcraft (Madrid: Sociedad General de Autores de España, 1992), 7.

2. Joaquín Rodrigo, "Memories of Composers I Have Known: Paul Dukas," unpublished lecture, trans. Katherine Zegarra. Ediciones Joaquín Rodrigo, 1998.

3. Victoria Kamhi, *Hand in Hand with Joaquín Rodrigo, My Life at the Maestro's Side*, trans. Ellen Wilkerson. (Pittsburgh: Latin American Literary Review Press, 1992), 83.

4. Cecilia Rodrigo, E-mail, October 29, 1998.

5. C. Rodrigo, E-mail, October 29, 1998.

6. Walter Starkie, *Spain: A Musician's Journey Through Time and Space*, 2 vols. (Geneva: Edisli, 1958), 263.

7. C. Rodrigo, E-mail, October 29, 1998.

8. C. Rodrigo, E-mail, October 29, 1998.

9. Richard Salem,"Blind Pianist Rodrigo Plays His Own Music," *Washington Post and Times Herald*, April 13, 1958, A(7).

10. *London Times*, "A Modern Spanish Composer," May 19, 1958, C(14).

11. *The Times*, "A Modern Spanish Composer," C(14).

12. Ivan March, "Beyond Aranjuez: Joaquín Rodrigo talks to Ivan March," *Gramophone*, 40 July 1992, 10-11.

13. C. Rodrigo, E-mail to author, 23 April 1998.

14. C. Rodrigo, E-mail, April 23, 1998.

15. C. Rodrigo, E-mail, April 23, 1998.

Chapter 2

Victoria Kamhi
and Her Life with Joaquín Rodrigo

The contributions of Victoria Kamhi to the career, quality of life, and opportunities made available to Maestro Rodrigo cannot be over-estimated. She served as a loving wife, an accomplished accompanist and pianist, poet, copyist, and revisionist of many of his works. According to Cecilia Rodrigo:

> The greatest part of her collaboration was in choosing texts for his songs, adapting them and translating them into English, French and German. On top of that, she was the most perfect multi lingual secretary, agent, public relations specialist, and advisor to my father on all of his contracts, almost like a lawyer. The files of of her correspondence are voluminous and she still had the time to accompany him to all of his social commitments and travels. She was an accomplished pianist as well. My father always emphasized the importance of her help.[1]

Maestro Rodrigo always composes in Braille and dictates the music note by note to a copyist. The transcription of a composition takes almost as much time as the composition process itself. Ms. Kamhi made the corrections between the copyist and the publisher.[2] Her biography, *Hand in Hand*, translated from the original Spanish by Ellen Wilkerson, gives great insight into her life "at the Maestro's

13

side."[3]

Victoria Kamhi was born in 1905 in Besiktas, a suburb of Constantinople. Her parents were Isaac Kamhi and Sofia Arditti, from Vienna. Isaac ran his father's very prosperous drug store chain, the Rafael Kamhi and Sons firm, traveling all over Europe to oversee its various branches. Victoria and her sister, Matilde, enjoyed the many opportunities that wealth brings.

Victoria showed early promise as a linguist, speaking Turkish, Spanish, French, German, and modern Greek as a very young child. She also had a musical gift, starting to play the piano by ear at only three and a half. She began studying with an Italian piano teacher at age seven, and at age ten, she auditioned for and was accepted as a pupil of Geza Heguey, a former student of Franz Liszt. Later, after her family moved to Vienna, Victoria studied with the Polish concert pianist and professor, Georg von Lalewicz. He required three hours of practice per day and two piano lessons a week. She made rapid progress and in her teens, accompanied singers, violinists, and other musicians. She attended many concerts available in Vienna--operas, recitals of famous pianists, violinists, ballets, and so forth.[4]

In 1918, the Kamhi family moved to Switzerland for health reasons and to escape the deprivations caused by World War I. Food and heating fuel were scarce. For about six months, they traveled as tourists to Zurich and Lucerne and later to Paris. In the summer of 1918, Isaac was appointed head of the Parisian branch of Rafael Kamhi and Sons, so the family moved to Paris. Professor Lalewicz soon followed the Kamhi's to Paris. Because he was unwilling to renounce his Polish citizenship, he lost his position at the Vienna Conservatory, and at almost fifty years of age, he was forced to rebuild his studio in a foreign city. Victoria, however, was happy for the opportunity to continue her studies with him, often practicing five hours a day. In the spring of 1920, Professor Lalewicz was offered a chair at the Buenos Aires Conservatory. He and his wife departed for the "new world," and he was appointed professor of the conservatory, where he trained many famous Spanish-American pianists.[5]

In 1920, Victoria began to prepare for admission to the Schola Cantorum. She successfully passed the piano audition and Vincent d'Indy, who presided over the audition, welcomed her to the schola. Unfortunately, Victoria did not pass into the advanced solfeggio class, and believing that enrollment into the elementary class would be a waste of her time, she decided not to enter. In retrospect, she felt this decision had been a mistake because in a short time she would have passed into the advanced class. The most difficult step was to gain admittance to the schola, an honor which she easily had won.[6]

After traveling to Salzburg on vacation, Victoria returned to Paris and began studying piano with Professor Lazare Lévy, who taught at the Paris Conservatory. She studied with him for five years and earned a diploma as a music teacher from the conservatory. She continued to be involved in the Parisian musical life, enjoying fine concerts and operas. The Kamhi financial situation took a disastrous turn in 1924 when the Kamhi firm declared bankruptcy. Victoria and Matilde became young ladies without dowries rather than promising young women with many opportunities. There were no more parties and fewer concerts, dinners, and vacations. But Victoria continued her studies, learning the Jacques Dalcroze rhythm method, and she took a state examination to receive accreditation to teach private piano lessons. In order to pass the test, administered by the Association des Prix de Piano du Conservatoire de Paris, she was required to perform a piano recital, take a written test in music history, and take a dictation test. Although Victoria passed with the grade "assez bien," this victory did not bring her concert engagements or students. In the meantime, she applied for other work without success.[7]

In 1929, Victoria met the young Valencian composer Joaquín Rodrigo through a friend studying at the Ecole Normale de Musique. Rodrigo had sent the score of *Cinco piezas infantiles* to a conductor of the Wiesbaden Orchestra and wanted the score returned. Letters in Spanish and French had been to no avail, so Victoria was asked to translate the letter into German. She had read of Rodrigo and was impressed with his *Preludio al gallo mañanero*. She looked forward to meeting the talented young composer, and a short time later, Rodrigo asked Victoria to attend the premiere of his *Cinco piezas infantiles*, performed by the Straram Orchestra. Rodrigo dedicated the work to her because her letter had successfully retrieved it from Germany. Of that premiere, she said:

> With the first measures of the *Cinco Piezas Infantiles* I was seized by a profound emotion: I held my breath so as not to miss a note. It was the *Plegaria*, pregnant with deep nostalgia, which most enraptured me. The audience's approval was unanimous, and the author was obliged to acknowledge their ovations several times from his box.[8]

Victoria and Joaquín continued their relationship, going to concerts together, playing the piano for each other, and enjoying poetry and nature together. Victoria's father, however, did not approve of their friendship because Joaquín had no viable means of supporting himself or a family. The two kept their meetings a secret for a few months until they decided that there was no hope of reconciling the situation. The two parted, with Joaquín returning to his family and Victoria working temporarily for the Rothschild Foundation as a social worker. Neither was happy, and Joaquín couldn't even compose because of his despair over the situation. So, as a result of their great love for each other and their despair over being separated, the two were married on January 19, 1933.[9]

The newly married couple were desperately poor and neither could find employment. After a year of marriage, the two separated for several months. Victoria went to Paris to see her family, and Joaquín stayed in Valencia. During the lonely separation, Joaquín managed to compose his award-winning *Per La Flor de Lliri Blau* and the song "Cántico de la esposa," of which he says:

> I regard my best vocal work to be "Cántico de la esposa," dedicated to my wife, where I believe I employed all my inspiration to express my sentiments towards her at a very difficult time of our life when, after just one year of marriage, we had to be separated for economic reasons. Far from her side, I wrote this song, set to a text by San Juan de la Cruz, the great Spanish mystic poet of the 16th century. In the Cántico, the esposa is the soul and a comparison is made between divine love and earthly love.[10]

In order to improve their financial situation, the Rodrigos became determined to win the Conde de Cartagena scholarship, the prestigious scholarship awarded by the Royal Academy of Fine Arts every two years to deserving musicians and painters. The two lobbied for votes among the academicians, including Manuel de Falla. It was Falla who succeeded in influencing the votes, and Joaquín was awarded the scholarship. After moving to Paris in March, 1935, Joaquín devoted himself to his work and quickly composed *Cuatro danzas de españa* and several songs, including "Coplas del pastor enamorado." Both Rodrigos attended classes at the Sorbonne and at the Ecole Normale de Musique that spring and in July 1935, they were named as correspondents for the Salzburg music festivals. They attended and critiqued many concerts, operas, ballets, and theatrical productions and made many important musical contacts. Their reviews were printed in *Le Monde Musical*.[11]

During this time, Joaquín completed his homage to Paul Dukas, several Spanish dances, and the song cycle, *Tríptic de Mosén Cinto*. Maestro Rodrigo considers this cycle to be one of his favorite works.[12]

When the Spanish Civil War broke out, the Rodrigo's faced a new challenge when the Academy of Fine Arts declared that all study grants were canceled, including the Conde de Cartagena. The two lived in Freiburg, Germany, at a home for the blind for a period of fifteen months. Joaquín spent the time practicing and composing, and Victoria practiced and worked at the home. They taught Spanish, read, went to concerts and operas, and the maestro presented a piano recital of his own compositions.

It was during this time that Rodrigo composed his "Canción del cucu" on a poem by Victoria. The trees in the Black Forest were filled with cuckoos, inspiring this collaborative effort. He also completed his *Cuatro piezas para piano: Plegaria de la infanta de Castilla, Fandango del Ventorrillo, Danza Valenciana* and *Caleseras.*[13]

In late summer, 1938, the Rodrigos moved to Paris hoping to better their financial situation. They socialized with many other Spaniards in exile--Roland-Manuel, composer and musicologist; María Cid, the Catalan singer; the composer Joaquín Nin-Culmell; the pianist Ricardo Viñes; the guitarists Emilio and Matilde Pujol, and others. Rodrigo had composed the second and third movements of his *Concierto de Aranjuez* by the spring of 1939. The tragedy of a stillborn daughter inspired the melancholy melody of the Adagio movement. Other themes were evoked by memories of their honeymoon as the Rodrigos strolled the park at Aranjuez.[14] The *Concierto de Aranjuez* made its jubilant and highly successful premier in November 1940. The concerto is still considered among the twelve best works of universal music literature, and its recordings are always best-sellers. Rodrigo himself later wrote a version for harp. The original work for guitar and orchestra was finally published in 1949.[15] When the composition was finally published, it was Victoria who prepared the score for publication and made corrections in the copy proofs. She also revised and corrected the *Concierto galante*, the cello concerto Rodrigo composed for Gaspar Cassadó. This task was especially difficult because Cassadó had ruined the original manuscript by cutting parts of the orchestral interludes.[16]

As the Spanish Civil War neared its conclusion, the Rodrigos received exciting news. Their Conde de Cartagena scholarship would be paid upon their return to Spain. Also, Manuel de Falla proposed that Rodrigo teach a music history class at either the University of Seville or the University of Granada. However, when Rodrigo was also offered the position of Musical Advisor for the Radio Nacional de España, he chose that position because the two preferred to live in Madrid. The Rodrigos reached Spain just two days before the outbreak of World War II.

After years of deprivation and near starvation, the Rodrigos were awarded many opportunities upon their return to Madrid. Joaquín was named chairman of art and publicity of the Spanish National Organiza-

tion for the Blind, a position he held for nearly thirty years. He was also named interim professor of folklore at the Royal Conservatory of Music. In 1940, Joaquín was hired as music critic for the newspaper *Pueblo*. Finally, the two could live in relative comfort without being forced to sell their belongings to have food on the table.[17]
Victoria, pregnant a second time, developed phlebitis. Juan Harguindey, a Madrid obstetrician, saved her life and the life of her baby. Joaquín was profoundly grateful and dedicated "Coplillas de Belén," the third of the *Villancicos* to Dr. Harguindey.[18]
Cecilia Rodrigo was born on January 27, 1941, and was baptized a few days later. Federico Sopeña, Rodrigo's biographer, and the singer Lola Rodríguez Aragón were pleased to serve as godparents.[19]
Rodrigo composed during this time his *Homenaje a la tempranica* and his *Gran marcha de los subsecretarios*, a composition for duo piano. Victoria and Joaquín included the latter on all of their tours-- in London, Paris, Puerto Rico, Caracas, Turkey, Japan, Portugal, and elsewhere.
In the mid-1940s, Victoria was commissioned by Radio Madrid to write short biographies on the love relationships of the great composers. Additionally, she wrote a biography of Edvard Grieg. When Joaquín accepted the invitation to offer a course on the history of music at the University in Oviedo, Victoria played musical examples at the piano. As Cecilia grew older, Victoria worked diligently as her husband's secretary, pianist, copyist, and companion, traveling with him all over the world.[20]
Although Maestro Rodrigo had lost most of his sight when he was only three, he retained some limited vision. Over the years, he was subject to acute infections in his eyes, causing fever and pain. In 1947, he suffered another infection, which took his remaining vision. Victoria wrote that following the crisis, he retained "his serene and optimistic nature," as is evidenced in his *Cuatro madrigales amatorios*. This song cycle premiered in February 1948, at the Círculo Medina and was sung by four young singers, all students of the great teacher Lola Rodríguez Aragón. The performance, accompanied by Maestro Rodrigo at the piano, was enormously popular. Also premiered that day was "Barcarole," Rodrigo's setting of Victoria's poem, which had been published in a Viennese magazine when she was only fifteen.[21]
The Rodrigos traveled extensively over the next few years. In August 1949, they set sail for Argentina and presented nineteen concerts in about five weeks. They visited England several times to present concerts and to be honored at world premieres of Rodrigo's works. In 1953, they made a professional tour to Morocco where Maestro Rodrigo played some of his compositions. They traveled to

Turkey that year to attend several "Rodrigo Festivals" and in 1957, traveled to Venezuela to attend the second Latin American Music Festival. This festival was organized to honor the most important composers of Spanish America, including Heitor Villa-Lobos, Alfonso Letelier, Blas Galindo, and others. The concerts were attended by diplomats, ambassadors, and leading musicians and writers of the day, among others. From there, they traveled to Puerto Rico to participate in the *Pablo Casals Festival*. Maestro Rodrigo presented a lecture that was followed by a concert of his works.[22]

In 1953, Victoria was commissioned to write the Spanish translation of Alban Berg's *Wozzeck*.[23] She continued accompanying, recording the Bach Flute Sonatas with the Valencian flautist Ribelles. She accompanied numerous performers in concert, including the singers Marími del Pozo, Isabel Penagos, and Conchita Badía, the Chilean violinist Pedro d'Andurain, and the violinist Angelina Verlasco. In 1954, Victoria wrote the story for Rodrigo's ballet, *Pavana real*, a plot honoring the great vihuelists of the sixteenth century. The work premiered in Barcelona in December 1955, with resounding success.[24] Ms. Kamhi became a member of the General Society of Spanish Authors as a writer and composer in 1956.[25]

Ms. Kamhi helped Joaquín select the themes to be used in *Fantasía para un gentilhombre*, a suite for guitar and chamber orchestra commissioned and dedicated to Andrés Segovia.[26] This work premiered in February 1958, in San Francisco, with Segovia and Enrique Jordá, conductor. The themes were melodies collected by Gaspar Sanz, the seventeenth-century guitarist in the court of King Felipe IV.[27] Ms. Kamhi translated for Maestro Rodrigo in interviews and for the lectures he presented prior to his concerts.

Because of her musical skill and facility with languages, Ms. Kamhi played a vital role in Rodrigo's life and career. It was to her that he dictated the cadenza in *Fantasía para un gentilhombre* so that the work could be published.[28] She translated many of his lectures and corrected the proofs for most of his compositions. She edited the *Concierto serenata* for piano and put in bowings and dynamics in the score to Rodrigo's 1963 lyric opera, *El Hijo fingido*.[29] Ms. Kamhi corrected the cantata *Música para un códice salmantino* and edited the *Album of Songs*. The list of her contributions to his work is immense. When Rodrigo was awarded the Grand Cross of Civil Merit in April 1966, he offered the cross to Vicky, because she "had helped him accomplish so much."[30]

Ms. Kamhi received many accolades, including the Ribbon of Alfonso the Wise in June 1977. She wrote that "it was proof that my work at Joaquín's side was recognized and appreciated."[31] In 1981, she was awarded the Gold Medal of the Red Cross of Spain, and that same year, she was awarded the Gold Medal of Mexico City, Mexico, for having saved her husband's life during a hotel fire. They were on the seventeenth floor, having arrived in Mexico City for the Rodrigo Festival and, although they lost all their clothing except what they were wearing, the two escaped harm.[32]

Ms. Kamhi was pleased to be named an adoptive daughter of the city of Sagunto, her husband's birthplace, in 1982. In 1991, she was presented the Noblelady's "Ribbon of Queen Isabella."[33]

As will be evidenced in this book, many of the song texts are original poems by Ms. Kamhi or adaptations by her of ancient, anonymous poems. No work regarding the life of Rodrigo would be complete without praise of Victoria Kamhi's contributions. Her influence, talent, and intelligence are an integral part of Joaquín Rodrigo's life and work.

Ms. Kamhi died July 21, 1997, in her sleep.

Notes

1. Cecilia Rodrigo, E-mail to author, April 23, 1998.
2. C. Rodrigo, E-mail to author, April 23, 1998.
3. Victoria Kamhi, *Hand in Hand with Joaquín Rodrigo, My Life at the Maestro's Side*, trans. Ellen Wilkerson (Pittsburgh: Latin American Literary Review Press, 1992).
4. Kamhi, *Hand in Hand*, 36.
5. Kamhi, *Hand in Hand*, 41.
6. Kamhi, *Hand in Hand*, 42.
7. Kamhi, *Hand in Hand*, 56.
8. Kamhi, *Hand in Hand*, 63.
9. Kamhi, *Hand in Hand*, 78.
10. C. Rodrigo, E-mail to author, April 23, 1998.
11. Kamhi, *Hand in Hand*, 88.
12. C. Rodrigo, E-mail to author, April 23, 1998.
13. Kamhi, *Hand in Hand*, 98.
14. Kamhi, *Hand in Hand*, 109.
15. C. Rodrigo, E-mail to author, October 29, 1998.
16. Kamhi, *Hand in Hand*, 144.
17. Kamhi, *Hand in Hand*, 111-112.
18. Kamhi, *Hand in Hand*, 112.
19. Kamhi, *Hand in Hand*, 117.
20. C. Rodrigo, E-mail to author, April 23, 1998.
21. Kamhi, *Hand in Hand*, 140.
22. Kamhi, *Hand in Hand*, 167.

23. Kamhi, *Hand in Hand,* 152.
24. Kamhi, *Hand in Hand,* 158.
25. Kamhi, *Hand in Hand,* 162.
26. Kamhi, *Hand in Hand,* 173.
27. Kamhi, *Hand in Hand,* 174.
28. Kamhi, *Hand in Hand,* 204.
29. Kamhi, *Hand in Hand,* 216.
30. Kamhi, *Hand in Hand,* 223.
31. Kamhi, *Hand in Hand,* 253.
32. Kamhi, *Hand in Hand,* 277.
33. Kamhi, *Hand in Hand,* 367.

Chapter 3

Canciones

This chapter includes all songs by Maestro Rodrigo that are not part of any cycle. There are twenty-three songs, in a variety of languages and styles, described below. The format is: the title or poetic line is given in International Phonetic Alphabet; the line in its original language then follows. The literal translation is the third line, stated in its original word order. When needed, a fourth line corrects the word order and improves the translation. Concluding each song is a program-ready, poetic translation. Opposite the song title is the duration of the song.

arɑ̃ʒyɛ ma pɑ̃seə
Aranjuez, ma pensée (1988)   3:45
Aranjuez, My Thought

Victoria Kamhi, poet
Vocal Range: B^3 to F^5
For voice and guitar

This song, like "En Aranjuez con tu amor," is an adaptation of the Adagio theme from the *Concierto de Aranjuez*. The marvelous video on the life of Joaquín Rodrigo, *"Shadows and Light:" Joaquín Rodrigo at 90/Concierto de Aranjuez*. Rhombus Media, Inc. (1993), dramatically demonstrates the immense popularity of the theme with the Spaniards. My experience also found this to be true. When I asked people in Sagunto if they could help me find the birthplace of Joaquín Rodrigo, many began to sing or hum this wonderful theme with the most joyous expression on their faces! The experience was very moving.

Because of the popularity of the concerto theme, however, several unscrupulous people made unauthorized transcriptions for various instruments or printed arrangements with texts. The Rodrigos initiated a lawsuit in 1967 to reclaim all rights to the melody, but lost.[1] In 1987, Cecilia Rodrigo sued again and won the rights to the theme. She encouraged Victoria to write French lyrics for guitar and voice. "Aranjuez ma pensée" was the result.[2]

aɾɑ̃ʒɛ mɛ ɛ la sezɔ̃ de rozə
Aranjuez, mai est la saison des roses,
May is the season of roses

su lə sɔlɛj ɛl sɔ̃ deʒa ekɔzə
sous le soleil elles sont déjà écloses,
under the sun they are already blooming

le maɲɔljazɑ̃ flœr sə pɑ̃ʃə
les magnolias en fleurs se penchent
the magnolias in bloom bend toward
(the blooming magnolias bend toward)

syr le zo klɛ dy taʒə
sur les eaux claires du Tage.
the waters clear of the Tagus River.
(the clear waters of the Tagus River)

e la nɥi sə park dø fwa sɑ̃tɛnɛrə
Et la nuit, ce parc deux fois centenaire
And the night, that park second time centenary
(And the night, the park's two hundredth anniversary)

sanimə sudɛ̃ ʃyʃɔtmɑ̃ e brɥisəmɑ̃ syptil aromə
s'anime soudain chuchotements, et bruissements, subtils arômes,
becomes animated suddenly whispering, and rustling, subtle aromas

kamɛnə lə vɑ̃ tavɛk dilystrə fɑ̃tomə
qu'amène le vent avec d'illustres fantômes.
that brings the wind with illustrious shadows.

œ̃ pɛ̃trə famø zavɛk sa palɛt maʒik
Un peintre fameux avec sa palette magique,
A painter famous with his palette magical
(A famous painter with his magical palette)

a sy kapte dimmɔrtɛl zimaʒə
a su capter d'immortelles images,
knew how to capture the immortal images,

lɔ̃brə dœ̃ rwa e dynə rɛnə
l'ombre d'un roi et d'une reine.
the shadow of a king and of a queen.

ɔr e tarʒã pɛrlə ze djamã fɛːtə sɔ̃ptyøzə
Or et argent, perles et diamants fêtes somptueuses
Gold and silver, pearls and diamonds festival magnificent
(Gold and silver, pearls and diamonds magnificent festival)

fam bɛlə ze vɔlyptøzə fjeːr kurtizã
femmes belles et voluptueuses fiers courtisans.
women beautiful and voluptuous, proud courtiers
(beautiful women and voluptuous, proud courtiers)

gitaːrə zo lwɛ̃ gitaːrə ze mãdɔlin zãtrə bɥisɔ̃
Guitares au loin, guitares et mandolines entre les buissons,
Guitars in the distance, guitars and mandolins among the thickets

ʒwœːr də flytə ʃãtœːr za lynisɔ̃
joueurs de flûte, chanteurs a l'unisson.
players of flute, singers at the unison.

mɔ̃ namuːr ʒə tə ʃɛrʃã vɛ̃ parmi le frɔ̃ːdə
Mon amour je te cherche en vain parmi les frondes
My love, I you look for in vain among the fronds
(My love, I look for you in vain among the fronds)

u tã də suvniːr vivasə zabɔ̃də de tã pase
où tant de souvenirs, vivaces abondent des temps passés,
where so many memories, long-lived (they) abound with time passed,

de ʒur zœɪ̃ø
des jours heureux.
of days happy.
(of happy days)

nu zavjɔ̃ vẽ tɑ̃ tu le dø
Nous avions vingt ans tous les deux.
We had twenty years both.
(We had twenty years to share)

Idiomatic translation:
Lovely Aranjuez, in May the roses bloom. Under the warm sun, they are already blooming. The magnolias are reflected in the clear water of the Tagus River. This park is two hundred years old, and at night, we are aware of whisperings, rustlings, subtle aromas, and ghosts that the wind brings. A famous painter, with his magical palette, knew how to capture immortal images of a king and a queen. Gold and silver, pearls and diamonds, the painter portrays a magnificent festival, with beautiful women and proud courtiers. We hear guitars and mandolins, flutes and singers from the bushes. My love, in vain I search for you among the fronds, where so many memories abound of times passed. We had twenty years to share.

ɛn aɾanxwɛθ kɔn tu amɔr
En Aranjuez con tu amor (1968)   3:40
(based on a theme from *Concierto de Aranjuez*)

Spanish adapted by Alfredo G. Segura
Vocal Range: B^3 to D^5
For voice and guitar

It was *Concierto de Aranjuez* that brought Maestro Rodrigo international fame in the 1940s. The *Concierto* was inspired by the 740 acres of lovely gardens that surround the Royal Palace (Palacio Real), the summer palace of the Spanish kings and queens since the time of Felipe II, (1556-1598).[3] The town, Aranjuez, is known for its strawberries and asparagus and is about an hour south of Madrid.

xunto a ti al pasar las ɔɾas
Junto a ti, al pasar las horas,
Next to you, to pass the hours,

ɔ mi amɔr aj un rumɔr
oh, mi amor, hay un rumor
oh, my love, there is a rumor

ðɛ fwɛntɛz ðɛ kristal
de fuentes de cristal
of fountains of crystal
(of crystal fountains)

kɛn ɛl xarðin paɾaθɛ aβlar
que en el jardin parece hablar
that in the garden seem to speak

ɛm bɔz βaxa laz rɔsas
en voz baja a las rosas.
in voice low to the roses.
(in a low voice to the roses.)

dulθɛ amɔr ɛsas ɔxas sɛkas
Dulce amor, esas hojas secas
Sweet love, these leaves dry
(Sweet love, these dry leaves)

siŋ kɔlɔr kɛ βarɛl βjɛntɔ
sin color que barre el viento
without color that sweeps the wind

sɔn rɛkwɛrðɔz ðɛ rɔmanθez ðɛ un ajɛr
son recuerdos de romances de un ayer,
are remembrances of romances of yesterday,

wɛʎaz ðɛ prɔmɛsas ɛtʃas kɔn amɔr
huellas de promesas hechas con amor,
impressions of promises made with love,

ɛn aɾanxwɛθ ɛntɾɛ un ɔmbɾɛ
en Aranjuez, entre un hombre
in Aranjuez, between a man

juna muxɛr ɛn un atarðɛθɛr
y una mujer en un atardecer
and a woman on one afternoon

kɛ sjɛmprɛ sɛ rɛkwɛrða
que siempre se recuerda.
that always will be remembered.

ɔ mjamɔr
Oh, mi amor,
Oh, my love,

mjɛntraz ðɔs sɛ kjɛɾan kɔn fɛrβɔr
mientras dos se quieran con fervor,
while two love each other with fervor,

nɔ ðɛxaɾan las flɔɾɛz ðɛ βɾɔtar
no dejarán las flores de brotar
not they will let the flowers to bud
(they will not let the flowers bud)

nia ðɛ faltar al mundɔ paθ
ni ha de faltar al mundo paz
nor will lack the world peace
(nor will the world lack peace)

ni kalɔr a la tjɛrra
ni calor a la tierra.
nor heat on the earth.

jɔ sɛ βjɛn kɛ aj palaβɾas wɛkas
Yo se bien que hay palabras huecas,
I know well that there are words hollow,
(I know well that there are hollow words,)

sin amɔr kɛ ʎɛβa ɛl βjɛntɔ
sin amor, que lleva el viento
without love, that take the wind

i kɛ naðjɛ las ɔjɔ kɔn atɛnθjɔn
y que nadie las oyó con atención,
and that no one listens to with attention,

pɛɾotɾas palaβɾas swɛnan
pero otras palabras suenan,
but other words sound,

ɔ mjamɔr
oh mi amor,
oh my love,

al kɔɾaθɔn kɔmɔ nɔtaz ðɛ kantɔ nupθjal
al corazón como notas de canto nupcial,
to the heart like notes of a nuptual song,

ja si tɛ kjɛɾɔ aβlaɾa sjɛn
ya si te quiero hablara si en.
now if I want you to speak.

aɾanxwɛz mɛspɛɾas
Aranjuez me esperas.
Aranjuez me you await.
(Aranjuez you await me.)

lwɛɣɔ al kaɛr ðɛ la tarðɛ
Luego al caer de la tarde
Later at the fall of the afternoon

sɛskutʃa un rumɔr
se escucha un rumor
is heard a rumor
(a rumor is heard)

jɛz la fwɛntɛ kɛ aʎi
y es la fuente que allí
and it is the fountain that there

paɾɛθɛ aβlar kɔn laz rosas
parece hablar con las rosas.
seems to speak with the roses.

ɛn aɾanxwɛθ kɔn tu amɔr
En Aranjuez, con tu amor.
In Aranjuez, with your beloved.

Idiomatic translation:
Being with you, love, is a wonderful way to pass the time. The fountains seem to speak in a low voice to the roses. The dry leaves that the wind sweeps are remembrances of yesterday's romances, promises of love. There is one afternoon in Aranjuez that will always be remembered. When a man and a woman love each other so deeply, the world will be at peace. Oh, my love, I know that there are hollow words without love, that the wind takes and that no one listens to with attention. Oh my love, like the notes of a bridal song, now if I want you to speak--Aranjuez, you await me.

barkaːrola
Barcarola (1948)   2:00
Barcarole

For Pilar Lorrengar
Victoria Kamhi, poet

Vocal Range: D^4 to $F^{\#5}$
For voice and piano

Victoria composed this poem when she was only fifteen and it was selected for publication in a Viennese magazine. The song premiered in 1948 on the same program with the premier of *Cuatro madrigales amatorios*.[4]

faːrə mʊntər klaenəs ʃɪflaen
Fahre munter, kleines Schifflein,
Go sprightly, little boat

glaetə dʊrç diː flut
gleite durch die flut,
glide through the high water,

klaːr ʔʊnt liːplɪç ʔɪst deːr hɪmːməl
klar und lieblich ist der Himmel,
clear and sweet is the heaven

ʔʊnt di: zeː geːt guːt
und die See geht gut.
and the sea goes well.

traː gə mɪç bɪs ʔan di: hyːtːə
Trage mich bis an die Hütte
I carry me to on the hut
(I go on to the hut)

vɑ ʔiç liːpçən fɪnt
wo ich Liebchen find,
where I sweet one find,
(where I find a sweet one,)

blaːzə du: di: vaesən zeː gəl
Blase du die weissen Segel,
Bubble you the white sail,
(Bubble white sail,)

frɪʃər guːtər vɪnt
frischer, guter Wind!
fresh, good wind.

faːrə mʊntər klaenəs ʃɪflaen
Fahre munter, kleines Schifflein,
Go sprightly, little boat,

zɛglə hɪmːməlvɛrts
segle himmelwärts
sail heavenwards

hɔyt drʏk ʔɪç maen hɔldər liːpçən
heut drück' ich mein holder Liebchen
today squeeze I my graceful sweetheart
(today I squeeze my graceful sweetheart)

fɛst fɛst ʔan maen hɛrts
fest, fest an mein Herz!
steadfast on my heart!

Idiomatic translation:
    Glide, my little boat, through the water and take me to visit my

sweetheart. Heaven is clear and sweet, the wind is fresh, and the sea is peaceful. Today, I will hold my beloved. Sail on, little boat.

kanθjɔn dɛl kuku
Cáncion del cucu (1937)   3:00
Song of the Cuckoo

For Alice van Walleghem
Victoria Kamhi, poet

Vocal Range: B^3 to D^5
For voice and piano

Maestro Rodrigo is fascinated by bird song and often uses the call of the cuckoo in his compositions.[5] The immature cuckoo sings a bird song of a major second, while in the adult bird, the song is the interval of a major third. Victoria considers this "one of his most beautiful and moving songs." [6]

kukliʎɔ kukliʎɔ kanta
Cuclillo, cuclillo canta,
Cuckoo, cuckoo sings,

dias sɔn dɛ kantar
días son de cantar,
days they are of song,
(the days are full of song,)

prɔntɔ ɛl duɾo θjɛrθɔ
pronto el duro cierzo
quickly the hard north wind

kɔrrɛ pɔr ɛl pinar
corre por el pinar.
passes for the pines.
(passes through the pines.)

dimɛ si ɔtɾɔz βɔskɛs
Dimé si otros bosques
Tell me if other woods

un dia jɔ βɛɾɛ
un día yo veré,
one day I will see,

si la lɛxana tjɛrra
si la lejana tierra
if the far-away lands

muj pɾɔntɔ aʎaɾɛ
muy pronto hallaré.
very quickly I will find.

di si pɔr ɛstɔz mundɔz
Dí si por estos mundos
Say if for these worlds

βaɣandɔ sjɛmpɾɛ irɛ
vagando siempre iré.
wandering always I will go
(I will always wander)

ɔ si mi βiða ɛrrantɛ
¿O si mi vida errante
Or if my life wandering
(Or if my wandering life)

muj pɾɔntɔ akaβaɾɛ
muy pronto acabaré?
very quickly will finish?

paxaɾɔ βwɛn paxaɾiʎɔ
Pájaro, buen pajarillo,
Bird, good little bird,

dimɛ si ɛz βɛrðað
díme si es verdad:
tell me if it is true:

ɛʎa ðiθɛ kɛ sjɛmpɾɛ
ella dice que siempre
she says that always

sjɛmpɾɛ mɛ sɛɣiɾa
siempre me seguirá...
always me she will follow...
(she will always follow me...)

kukliʎɔ kukliʎɔ kanta
¡Cuclillo, cuclillo canta!
Cuckoo, cuckoo sing!

Idiomatic translation:
     The cuckoo sings every morning, and the hard north wind moves through the pines. Tell me if I will see other woods and far-away lands. Tell me if I will always wander, little bird, or if my wandering days will soon end. Good bird, tell me if what she says is true. Will she always follow me?

kanθjɔn dɛl ɣɾumɛtɛ
Canción del grumete (1938)   1:35
Song of the Cabin Boy

For Lola Rodriguez de Aragón
Anonymous poet

Vocal Range: E^4 to E^5
For voice and piano

     This song was composed for a movie on the life of Christopher Columbus, which unfortunately, was never produced. However, "Canción del grumete" was such a popular song, it was later performed frequently by Spanish singers.[7]

ɛn la mar aj una tɔrrɛ
En la mar hay una torre,
In the sea there is a tower,

jɛn la tɔrrɛ una βɛntana
y en la torre una ventana
and in the tower a window

jɛn la βɛntana una niɲa
y en la ventana una niña
and in the window a girl

kɛ a lɔz maɾinɛɾɔz ʎama
que a los marineros llama.
that to the sailors she calls.
(who calls to the sailors.)

pɔr aʎi βjɛnɛ mi βarkɔ
Por allí viene mi barco,
Over there it comes my boat,
(From there comes my boat,)

kɛ lɔ kɔnɔθkɔ ɛn la βɛla
que lo conozco en la vela,
that I know in the sail,
(I know its sail,)

jɛn ɛl palɔ majɔr ʎɛβa
y en el palo mayor lleva
and in the mast highest it carries away
(and in the highest mast it carries)

lɔz riθɔz ðɛ mi mɔɾena
los rizos de mi morena.
the curls of my dark-haired girl.

Idiomatic translation:
In the sea, there is a tower and in the tower, there is a window. From the window, a girl calls to the sailors. My boat is coming! I can recognize it by its sail! In the highest mast, it carries the curls of my dark-haired girl.

kantiθɛl
Canticel (1935)   1:30
Song

Josep Carner, poet

Vocal Range: D^4 to E^5
For voice and piano

This song is excerpted from the cycle, *Cuatre cançons en llengua catalana,* and is included with both Catalan and Castilian texts in the Schott edition of *35 Songs for Voice and Piano.* Gerardo Diego adapted the original poem by Josep Carner. Here, I have transcribed the Castilian text into IPA. The Catalan text is transcribed with the cycle, in Chapter 7.

pɔr una βɛla ɛn lalta mar
Por una vela en la alta mar
For a sail on the high sea

daɾia un tɾɔnɔ
daria un trono,
I would give a throne,

pɔr una βɛla ɛn lalta mar
por una vela en la alta mar
for a sail on the high sea

aθul dɛl mar
azul del mar.
blue of the sea.

pɔr βɛr ɛl rɔstɾɔ a una βirtuð
Por ver el rostro a una virtud
To see the face of a virtue

mi ɣɔθɔ ðjɛɾa
mi gozo diera
my joy I would give

i mɛθjɔ rɔta ɛm mi lauð
y medio rota en mi laud,
and half broken in my lute,

mi xuβɛntuð
mi juventud.
my youth.

pɔr una flɔr ðɛl βɛrðɛ aβɾil
Por una flor del verde abril
For a flower of green April

mjamɔr pɛrŏjɛɾa
mi amor perdiera
my love I would lose

pɔr una flɔr ŏɛl βɛrŏɛ aβɾil
por una flor del verde abril
for a flower of green April

mjamɔr pɛrŏi
mi amor perdi...
my love I lost...

Idiomatic translation:
    I would give my throne for a sail on the high seas. To see a virtuous face, I would give my joy and my youth. For an April flower, I would lose the one I love. For an April flower, I lost the one I love.

kantikɔ ŏɛ la ɛspɔsa
Cántico de la esposa (1934)   4:12
Song of the Bride

To Victoria Kamhi
San Juan de la Cruz, poet

Vocal Range: C^4 to A^5
For voice and piano

    Rodrigo regards this as his best vocal work, as quoted on page 16, Chapter 2.
    San Juan de la Cruz (1542-1591), born in Fontiveros, Avila, studied at Salamanca University and became the spiritual advisor to the Saint Teresa Convent in Avila. He spent almost a year in jail in Toledo in 1577 for his reform movement of the Carmelite Order, during which time, he wrote three poems. These poems made him immortal in mystic literature: *Canciones del alma en la íntima comunicación de unión de amor de Dios, Canciones entre el alma y el esposa,* and *Noche oscura.* All of his poetry and prose illustrate the way to a perfect union of the human soul with God. De la Cruz compares the joys of spiritual love with symbolic references to carnal love. He was beatified in 1675 and canonized in 1726.[8]

a ðɔndɛ tɛskɔndistɛ
¿A dónde te escondiste
To where did you hide yourself,
(Where did you hide,)

amaðɔ i mɛ ðɛxas tɛ kɔŋ xɛmiðɔ
amado, y me dejas te con gemido?
loved one, and to me you left with groan?
(loved one, and you left me groaning?)

kɔmɔ ɛl θjɛɾβɔ wistɛ
Como el ciervo huíste,
How like the deer you ran away,

aβjɛndɔmɛ fɛɾiðɔ
habiéndome ferido;
wounding me;

sali tɾas ti klamandɔ i ja ɛɾas iðɔ
salí tras tí clamando, y ya eras ido.
I went after you crying, and already you were gone.

pastɔɾɛz lɔs kɛ fwɛɾɛðɛs
Pastores, los que fuéredes,
Shepherds, those who snared,

aʎa pɔr laz maxaðas al ɔtɛɾɔ
allá por las majadas al otero,
over there by the sheep-folds at the knoll,

si pɔr βɛntuɾa βjɛɾɛðɛs
si por ventura viéredes,
if perhaps you should see,

akɛl kɛ jɔ mas kjɛɾɔ
aquel que yo más quiero,
he that I most love,

ðɛθiðlɛ kɛ aðɔlɛθkɔ pɛnɔj mwɛɾɔ
decidle que adolezco, peno y muero.
tell him that I suffer, pain and die.

buskandɔ mis amɔɾɛs
Buscando mis amores,
Looking for my loves,

iɾɛ pɔr ɛsɔz mɔntɛs i riβɛɾas
iré por esos montes y riberas;
I will go to those mountains and shores;

ni kɔxɛɾɛ flɔɾɛs
ni cogeré las flores,
neither will I take the flowers

ni tɛmɛɾɛ las fjɛɾas
ni temeré las fieras
nor will I fear the wild beasts

i pasaɾɛ lɔs fwɛrtɛs i fɾɔntɛɾas
y pasaré los fuertes y fronteras.
and I will pass the fortress and frontiers.

ɔ βɔskɛs jɛspɛsuɾas
¡Oh bosques y espesuras,
Oh forests and thickets,

plantaðɔs pɔr la manɔ ðɛl amaðɔ
plantados por la mano del Amado!
planted by the hand of the beloved!

ɔ pɾaðɔ ðɛ βɛrðuɾas
¡Oh prado de verduras,
Oh meadow of greenery,
(oh, green meadow,)

dɛ flɔɾɛs ɛzmaltaðɔ
de flores esmaltado,
of flowers enameled,
(of enameled flowers,)

dɛθið si pɔr βɔsɔtɾɔs a pasaðɔ
decid si por vosotros ha pasado!
say if for you he has passed!

Idiomatic translation:
  Why did you leave me, beloved? Like a deer, you ran away, leaving me wounded. I was crying as I looked for you, but you were already gone. Shepherd on the hills, if you see my beloved, tell him that I am suffering and that I am dying. I will go look for my love in the mountains and at the shores. I will not stop to pick flowers, nor will I be afraid of wild animals as I pass through the frontiers. Oh forests that were planted by my beloved. Oh flowers, tell me if he passed by you.

la ʃãsɔ̃ də ma vi
La Chanson de ma vie (1939)   3:50
The Song of My Life

Juan Camp, poet
Vocal Range: A^3 to F^5
For voice and piano

  This song, like "Chimères," (pages 43-47) is popular in nature and was composed in the late 1930s while the Rodrigos were living in Paris. Both songs were composed in the hopes that they would make money for the Rodrigos, who were living in poverty at the time. Joaquín wrote sentimental song settings for the two French "nightclub" songs, "Chimères" and "La Chanson de ma vie."[9]

pur mjø tə fɛ: rɑtãdrə
Pour mieux te faire entendre
For better you make to understand
(To help you better understand)

sɛttə bɛrsøːzə tã:drə
cette berceuse tendre
this cradle tender
(this cradle song)

kə mɔ̃ kœ: rã nemwa
que mon coeur en émoi,
that my heart in emotion,

dã sa ʒwa avɛ rɛveə puːr twa
dans sa joie avait revée pour toi,
in its joy has dreamed for you,

ʒavɛ dɑ̃ zœ̃ pɔɛːmə
j'avais dans un poème
I have in a poem

avue kə ʒə tɛmə
avoué que je t'aime
confessed that I you love
(confessed that I love you)

e ma lɛvra mi vwa
et ma lèvre à mi-voix
and my lips at half-voice

tə myrmyrɛ ravi
te murmurait ravie
to you I would murmur enraptured

la ʃɑ̃sɔ̃ də ma vi
la chanson de ma vie.
the song of my life.

dɔːtrə vjɛ̃drɔ̃ sɑ̃ dutə
D'autres viendront sans doute
The others will come without doubt

myrmurə syːr ta rutə
murmurer sur ta route
murmuring on your way

tu sɛ mɔ karɛsɑ̃
tous ces mots caressants
all the words caressing
(all the caressing words)

dɔ̃ laksɑ̃ tɑ̃flaməra mɔ̃ sɑ̃
dont l'accent enflammera mon sang.
in the tone that enflames my blood.

e puːr dɑtrə mɛtrɛsə
Et pour d'autre maitresses
And for other sweethearts

ty fɥi ze mə delɛsə
tu fuis et me délaisses
you flee and me abandon
(you flee and abandon me)

e twa disparɛsɑ̃
et toi disparaissant
and you vanished

alɔ:r sɛra fini
alors sera finie
then will be finished

la ʃɑ̃sɔ̃ də ma vi
la chanson de ma vie.
the song of my life.

Refrain

lə ʒu:r u ʒə ʃɑ̃tɛ pu:r twa
Le jour où je chantais pour toi
The day when I will sing for you

te zjø brijɛ də ply flɑ:m
tes yeux brillaient de plus flamme
your eyes brilliant of more flame
(your eyes brilliant with flame)

e ʒə sɑ̃tɛ vibre dɑ̃ tɔ̃ namə
et je sentais vibrer dans ton âme
and I feel vibrate in your soul

œ̃ du zɛmwa mɛ rjɛ̃ nə fɥi ply kə lamu:r
un doux èmoi. Mais rien ne fuit plus que l'amour
a sweet emotion. But nothing flees more than the love

dy kœ:r də lɔ mu də la fam
du coeur de l'homme ou de la femme
in the heart of the man or of the woman

lə tã dɛme parɛ trɔ kuːr tuʒuːr
le temps d'aimer parait trop court toujour.
the time of love appears too short always.

mɔ̃ kœːr ʒamɛ nubliə
Mon coeur jamais n'oublie
My heart never will forget

la ʃãsɔ̃ də ma vi
la chanson de ma vie.
the song of my life.

Idiomatic translation:
To help you better understand this cradle song that my emotional heart has dreamed for you, I have written a poem in which I confessed my love for you. To you, I would murmur the song of my life. Other lovers will come, without a doubt, murmuring sweet words to you. You will leave me for them, and the song of my life will be finished.
One day, I will sing for you and your eyes will be brilliant. I will feel your soul vibrate with sweet emotion. But love flees quickly from the heart of a man or woman, and the time of love is always short. My heart will never forget the song of my life.

ʃimɛːrə
Chimères (1939)   5:00
Myth

Text by Victoria Kamhi
Vocal Range: $C^{\#}4$ to D^5

For voice and piano

Like "La Chanson de ma vie," "Chiméres" is a popular song written during the time the Rodrigos lived in Paris.

œ̃ namuːr sã rətuːr
Un amour sans retour
A love without return

mɑ̃lɛv tu ia ʒwa də vivrə
m'enlève toute la joie de vivre.
to me removes all the joy of living.
(removes my joy of living.)

y nimɑʒə ki mɑ̃nivrə
Une image qui m'enivre
An image that to me intoxicates
(an image the intoxicates me)

rɑ̃pli tu me nɥi
remplit toutes mes nuits
occupies all my nights

ʃarʒe dɛ̃sɔmni
chargées d'insomnie.
burdened with insomnia.

ʒə tə vwa sɑ̃ sɛsə
Je te vois sans cesse
I you see without ceasing
(I see you incessantly)

o bra dyn mɛtrɛsə
au bras d'une maîtresse.
in the arm of a sweetheart.
(in the arms of a sweetheart.)

ta mɛ̃ la karɛsə
Ta main la caresse,
Your hand her caresses,
(You caress her,)

ty pas ʒə tə sɥi də ma fənɛ:trə
tu passes, je te suis de ma fenêtre
you pass, I you am from my window
(I see you from my window)

ʒyska tə vwa:r disparɛ:trə
jusqu'à te voir disparaître
until to you see disappear
(and then you disappear)

ɛ̃sɑ̃sibɫə frwa te distɑ̃
insensible, froid et distant.
insensitive, cold and distant.

e purtɑ̃ dɑ̃ lə tɑ̃
Et pourtant dans le temps,
And yet in the time,

ty mavɛ bjɛ̃ di ʒə tɛmə
tu m'avais bien dit "je t'aime."
you to me have well said "I you love."
(you have said "I love you.")

ty mə ʃɑ̃tɛ te pɔɛːmə
Tu me chantais tes poèmes,
You me would sing your poems,
(You would sing to me your poems,)

o sɔ̃ lɑ̃gurø
aux sons langoureux
with sounds languorous
(with the languorous sounds)

dɑ̃ bɑ̃ʒo kaprisjø
d'un banjo capricieux.
of a banjo whimsical.
(of a whimsical banjo)

ʒɑ̃tɑ̃ te parɔlə
J'entends tes paroles,
I hear your words,

tɔ̃ nalɛn mə frolə
ton haleine me frôle,
your breath me brushes past,
(your breath brushes past me)

ʒə trɑ̃blə ʒə mafɔl
je tremble, je m'affole.
I tremble, I panic.

ɔ twa sə pøtil kə ty ubliə
Ô toi, se peut-il que tu oublies
Oh you, is it possible that you forget

lə du sɛrmã ki nu li
le doux serment qui nous lie,
the sweet promise that us binds,
(the sweet promise that binds us,)

ki nu li pur tuʒuːr
qui nous lie pour toujours?
that us will bind for always?
(that will bind us forever?)

nyl ɛspwaːr də tə vwaːr
Nul espoir de te voir.
No hope of you seeing.
(No hope of seeing you.)

mɔ̃ kœːr trist mə rekɔ̃fɔrtə
Mon coeur triste me réconforte.
My heart sad me comforts.
(My sad heart comforts me.)

ty fɥi dyrəmã ma pɔrtə
Tu fuis durement ma porte,
You flee roughly my door,
(You flee roughly from my door,)

vɔla ʒamã dœ̃ tro kuː rɛ̃stã
volage amant d'un trop court instant.
fickle lover of a too short instance.
(fickle lover of a short time.)

kə fotil dɔ̃ːk fɛːrə
Que faut-il donc faire
Is it necessary then to make

puː rãkɔːr tə plɛːr
pour encore te plaire
for again to you please
(again to please you)

ɔ ma dusə ʃimɛːrə
o ma douce chimère?
oh my sweet myth?

di mwa si mɔ̃ kɔr suplə də bakɑ̃tə
Dis-moi, si mon corps souple de bacchante
Tell me if my body yielding of leud woman
(Tell me if my leud, yielding woman's body)

si tutə ma ʒœnɛ sardɑ̃
si toute ma jeunesse ardente
if all my youth ardent
(if all my ardent youth)

nə mɛritə ply tɔ̃ bɛze
ne méritent plus ton baiser.
no merit more your kiss.
(doesn't merit your kiss anymore.)

Idiomatic translation:
A love without return takes away all the joy of life. The image that intoxicates me also keeps me awake all night. I see you in the arms of another. Your hand caresses her, and then you pass by my window. I watch until you disappear, insensitive, cold, and distant.

And yet, you have said you love me. You would sing me your poems with the languorous sounds of a whimsical banjo. I hear your words and feel your breath. I tremble and panic. How is it possible that you can forget the sweet promise that binds us, that will bind us, forever?

I have no hope of seeing you. My sad heart comforts me. You run from my door, fickle lover. How can I please you, sweet myth? Tell me if my willing body and ardent youth don't merit more than your kiss.

kɔplaz ðɛl pastɔr ɛnamɔɾaðɔ
Coplas del pastor enamorado (1935)   3:15
Verses of the Shepherd Enamored
(The Enamored Shepherd's Verses)

For Aurelio Veñas
Lope de Vega, poet

Vocal Range: B^3 to G^5
For voice and piano

Lope Felix de Vega Carpio (1562-1635), born in Madrid, is considered the outstanding dramatist of the Spanish Golden Age. He began dictating poetry at age five, before he could write. Vega was educated at the Jesuits' School in Madrid and later studied at the Academia Real.

Vega wrote more than two thousand plays, as well as epic poems, lyric poems, novels, epistles, short stories, and sonnets. Unfortunately, only about five hundred of his works are extant. The sheer magnitude of his output is astounding, and his talent, plus his scandalous life, practically made him a legend in his own lifetime. He is credited with having created a national drama for Spain as Shakespeare did for England.[10]

bɛrðɛz riβɛɾas amɛnas
Verdes riberas amenas,
Green banks pleasant,
(Pleasant green banks,)

fɾɛskɔs i flɔɾiðɔz βaʎɛs
frescos y floridos valles,
fresh and flowering valleys,

aɣwas puɾas kɾistalinas
aguas puras, cristalinas,
waters pure, cristaline,

altɔz mɔntɛz ðɛ kjɛn naθɛn
altos montes de quién nacen.
high mountains from which they are born.

giaðmɛ pɔr βwɛstɾas sɛndas
Guiadme por vuestras sendas
You lead me along your paths

i pɛrmitiðmɛ kɛ aʎɛ
y permitidme que halle
and permit me that I may find

εsta pɾεnda kε pεrði
esta prenda que perdí,
this pledge that I lost,

i mε kwεsta amɔr taŋ gɾandε
y me cuesta amor tan grande.
and me costs love so great.
(and costs me so great a love.)

Ʌεβɔ tεɲiðas εn saŋgɾε
Llevo, teñidas en sangre,
It carries, stained in blood,

las aβarkas i laz manɔs
las abarcas y las manos,
the sandals and the hands,

rɔtaz ðε apartar xaɾalεs
rotas de apartar jarales;
broken from removing thorns from rockroses;

dε ðɔrmir sɔβɾε laɾεna
de dormir sobre la arena
from sleeping on the sand

dε akεʌa ðεsjεrta marxεn
de aquella desierta margen,
by that deserted edge,

tɾajyɔ εnetɾaðɔ εl kaβεʌɔ
traigo enhetrado el cabello,
I bring entangled the hair,
(I bring entangled hair,)

i kwandɔ εl auɾɔɾa salε
y cuando el aurora sale,
and when the dawn emerges,

mɔxaðɔ pɔr εl rɔθiɔ
mojado por el rocío
moist from the dew

kɛ pɔr mi kaβɛθa ɛsparθɛn
que por mi cabeza esparcen
that by my head spread

laz nuβɛs kɛ ðɛl sɔl ujɛn
las nubes que del sol huyen
the clouds that from the sun escape

umɛðɛθjɛndɔ lɔs ajɾɛs
humedeciendo los aires.
moistening the air.

bɛrðɛz riβɛɾas amɛnas
Verdes riberas amenas,
Green banks pleasant,
(Pleasant green banks,)

fɾɛskɔs i flɔɾiðɔz βaʎɛs
frescos y floridos valles,
fresh and flowering valleys,

aɣwas puɾas kɾistalinas
aguas puras, cristalinas,
waters pure, crystalline,

altɔz mɔntɛz ðɛ kjɛn naθɛn
altos montes de quién nacen...
high mountains from which they were born...

Idiomatic translation:
   Pleasant green banks, flowering valleys, and pure water born of high mountains, guide me along your paths and allow me to find my lost promise that cost me my love. I sleep on the deserted sand with sandals and hands broken from the thorns of rock roses. My entangled hair is wet from the dew and above my head, clouds flee from the sun. Pleasant green banks, flowering valleys, and pure water born of high mountains...

la ɛspɛɾa
La espera (1952)   3:00
The Expectation

Victoria Kamhi, poet
Vocal Range: E^4 to Ab^5

For voice and piano or voice and orchestra

Orchestra--flute, English horn, harp, strings

"La espera" is #5 of *Villancicos y canciones de navidad* for soprano, chorus, and orchestra, but is published separately. It is sometimes performed with *Tres villancicos*–in this order, "La espera," "Aire y donaire," "Coplillas de Belén," and "Pastorcito Santo"--and called *Cuatro villancicos*. [11]

kwandɔ ʎeɣɛ aj jɔ nɔ sɛ
Cuando llegue, ay, yo no sé.
When does he arrive, oh, I no know.
(When does he arrive, oh, I do not know.)

pɔr kɛ lɛ teŋgɔ kɛ ɔkultar pɔr kɛ
¿por qué le tengo que ocultar, por qué?
why him must I conceal, why?
(why must I conceal him, why?)

nɔ kanta nɔ ɛl xilɣeɾo
¿No canta, no el jilguero
No he sings, no the finch
(Does he not sing, the finch)

kɛ reɣɾɛsal tiβjɔ niðɔ
que regresa al tibio nido
that he returns to the warm nest
(when he returns to his warm nest)

kwandɔ ɛl dia ja sɛ a iðɔ
cuando el día ya se ha ido?
when the day already it has gone?
(at the end of the day?)

peɾo jɔ tristɛ ɛspeɾo
Pero yo, triste, espero...
But I, sad, hope....

dimɛlɔ aj aβɛθɪʎa tu
Dímelo, ay, avecilla tú.
Tell me, oh, little bird you.
(Tell me, oh, you little bird.)

pɔr kɛ tɛnɛmɔs kɛ wir pɔr kɛ
¿por qué tenemos que huir, por qué?
why must we flee, why?

dimɛlɔ tu la fwɛntɛ
Dímelo tú, la fuente,
Tell me you, the fountain,
(Tell me, fountain,)

la kɛ βrɔtaz ðɛ la ɛntraɲa
la que brotas de la entraña
she that springs up from the interior
(as you spring from underground)

dɛsa aɾiða mɔntaɲa
de esa árida montaña,
from that arid mountain,

kɾistalinaj tɾanspaɾɛntɛ
cristalina y transparente.
crystaline and transparent.

dimɛlɔ pwɛs jɔ nɔ lɔ sɛ
Dímelo, pues yo no lo sé,
Tell me, becauses I no it know,
(Tell me, because I do not know it,)

pɔr kɛ tɛnɛmɔs kɛ wir pɔr kɛ
¿por qué tenemos que huir, por qué?
why must we flee, why?

ixɔ ðɛl alβɔraða
Hijo del alborada,
Son of the dawn,

luθεɾitɔ kɛ jɔ βi
lucerito que yo ví,
little bright star that I saw,

dimεlɔ si paɾa mi εm bɛlεn
dimelo si para mí en Belén
tell me what for me in Bethlehem
(tell me what is there for me in Bethlehem)

aβɾa εsta nɔtʃε pɔsaða
¿habrá esta noche posada?
will there be this one night lodging?
(will there be lodging this one night?)

dimεlɔ pɔr tu fε
Dímelo, por tu fé,
Tell me, for your faith,

pɔr kɛ tεnεmɔs kɛ wir pɔr kɛ
¿Por qué tenemos que huir, por qué?
Why must we flee, why?

εskutʃamε sεɲɔr
Escúchame, Señor,
Listen to me, sir,

nɔ mε aβandɔnas tu lɔ sɛ
no me abandonas Tú, lo sé,
no me will abandon You, I know,
(You will not abandon me, I know,)

kɔŋfiaða kaminaɾε
confiada caminaré,
trusting, I will walk,

um pɔrtal nɔ a ðε faltar
un portal no ha de faltar...
a portal no it has of lacking...
(a portal does not have to be lacking...)

dɛ tu manɔ si firmɛ iɾɛ fɛliθ
De tu mano, sí firme iré feliz,
From your hand, yes resolute I will go, happy,

un sɔl a ðɛ naθɛr lɔ sɛ
un sol ha de nacer, lo sé.
a sun must be born, I know.

ɔ βɛn niɲɔ ðiβinɔ
¡Oh ven, Niño divino!
Oh come, Boy divine!

Idiomatic translation:
When does he arrive, oh, I do not know. Why must I conceal him? Doesn't the finch sing when returning to his warm nest as night falls? I am sad. Tell me, little bird, why must we flee? Fountain, tell me, tell me why we must flee. Son of the dawn, little bright star, tell me if there will be lodging this night in Bethlehem. Tell me, for your faith, why must we flee? Listen to me, Lord. I know you will not abandon me, I will trust in you. Your hand will lead me for I know a sun must be born. Oh come, Boy divine!

ɛsta niɲa sɛ ʎɛβa la flɔr
Esta Niña se lleva la flor (1934)   1:25
This Girl Carries the Flower

To Conchita Supervia
Francisco de Figueroa, poet

Vocal Range: $C^{\#4}$ to B^{b5}
For voice and piano

Francisco de Figueroa, born in Alcalá, was called "el Divino" in his lifetime. He was a friend of Miguel de Cervantes, who praised him in the *Galatea*. Figueroa studied in Italy, writing poetry in both Castilian and Italian. His works, with themes of nature, love, and solitude, are remembered for their use of imagination and their fluid style.[12]

Conchita Supervia enjoyed an international singing career in the 1920s and 1930s.

εsta niɲa sε ʎεβa la flɔr
Esta niña se lleva la flor,
This girl carries the flower

kε las ɔtraz nɔ
que las otras no.
that the others not.
(that the others do not.)

εsta niɲa εrmɔsa
Esta niña hermosa,
This girl lovely,
(This lovely girl,)

kujɔz riθɔs sɔn
cuyos rizos son
whose curls are

la kuna εŋ kεl dia
la cuna en que el día
the cradle that the day

sε rεkwεstal sɔl
se recuesta al sol,
lays rest in the sun,

kuja βlaŋka fɾεntε
cuya blanca frente
whose white forehead

la auɾɔɾa nεβɔ
la aurora nevó
the dawn snows

kɔm bɾuɲiðɔs kɔpɔz
con bruñidos copos
with shiny snowflakes

ðε su βlaŋkɔ umɔr
de su blanco humor,
of her white humor,

pwɛs ɛŋ kwɛrpɔj manɔs
pues en cuerpo y manos
thus in body and hands

tal manɔ lɛ ðjɔ
tal mano le dió
such hand to him she gave

dɛ karmin nɛβaðɔ
de carmín nevado
of crimson snow

kwal nuŋka sɛ βjɔ
cual nunca se vió.
which never has been seen.

ɛsta niɲa sɛ ʎɛβa la flɔr
¡Ah! Esta niña se lleva la flor,
Ah! This girl carries the flower,

kɛ las ɔtraz nɔ
que las otras no.
that the others not.
(that the others do not.)

arkɔs sɔn sus θɛxas
Arcos son sus cejas
Arches (bows) are her eyebrows

kɔŋ kɛ jɛɾɛ amɔr
con que hiere Amor,
with which wounds love,
(with which love wounds,)

kɔn tan linda βista
con tan linda vista
with such good aim

kɛ a niŋgunɔ ɛrrɔ
que a ninguno erró.
that it not one missed.
(that never missed.)

kanɛlaj aθukar
Canela y azúcar
Cinnamon and sugar

suz mɛxiʎas sɔn
sus mejillas son,
her cheeks are,

j kjɛn laz ðiβiðɛ
y quien las divide,
and who them divides,
(and who [the nose] divides them,)

ðɛ lɛtʃɛj arrɔθ
de leche y arroz.
of milk and rice.

nɔ ɛz naða la βɔka
No es nada la boca,
No it is nothing the mouth,
(Her mouth is nothing,)

pɛɾɔ aʎjɛŋkɔntɾɔ
pero allí encontró
but there did find

sus pɛrlaz lauɾɔɾa
sus perlas la aurora,
her pearls the dawn,

su kɔɾal ɛl sɔl
su coral el sol.
her coral the sun.

ɛsta niɲa sɛ ʎɛβa la flɔr
¡Ah! Esta niña se lleva la flor,
Ah! This girl carries the flower,

kɛ las ɔtraz nɔ
que las otras no.
that the others not.
(that the others do not.)

Idiomatic translation:
    This girl carries the flower that the others do not. Her curls are the cradle in which the day lays rest to the sun. Dawn snows on her white forehead. She will give to him a crimson hand, which he has never seen. Ah, this girl is carries the flower that the others do not. Her eyebrows are like the wounding arrows of love. Her cheeks are cinnamon and sugar and her nose is pure, like milk and rice. Dawn has found its pearls in her mouth, and the sun found its coral there. This girl is taking the flower that the others do not.

ɛstriβiʎɔ
Estribillo (1934)   :55
Refrain

For Angeles Otein
S. J. Polo de Medina

Vocal Range: A^4 to E^6
For voice and piano

    Salvador Jacinto Polo de Medina (1603-1676), born in Murcia, was a poet and a writer of fables. Ordained as a priest, he wrote poems about nature, socio-literary commentary, and humorous fables.[13]
    Angeles Otein, born in 1895, was an international opera singer and taught many fine singers in the 1940s and 1950s. Her student Marimí del Pozo premiered many songs of Maestro Rodrigo.[14]

i mwɛɾa jɔ ðɛ amɔr pɔr pɛɾinarða
Y muera yo de amor por Perinarda,
And may die I of love for Perinarda,
(And may I die of love for Perinarda,)

dɛzðɛ kɛ naθɛl sɔl asta kɛ paɾa
desde que nace el sol hasta que para.
from that is born the sun until it sets.
(from whence the sun is born until it sets.)

kantɛn las aβɛs swɛnɛn laz ramas
Canten las aves, suenen las ramas,
They will sing the birds, sound the branches,
(Let the birds sing, let the branches sound,)

i lɔs paxariʎɔs tiplɛs alaðɔs
y los pajarillos, tiples alados,
and the little birds, soprano winged,
(and the little birds, winged sopranos,)

kantɛn arpaðɔs a swɛnɛn sɔnɔɾɔs
canten arpados, ah, suenen sonoros
they will sing melodiously, ah, sound loudly

ɛn swaβɛs kɔɾɔs
en suaves coros.
in the gentle chorus.

i mwɛɾa jɔ ðɛ amɔr pɔr pɛɾinarða
Y muera yo de amor por Perinarda,
And may die I of love of Perinarda,
(And may I die of love for Perinarda,)

dɛzðɛ kɛ naθɛl sɔl asta kɛ paɾa
desde que nace el sol hasta que para.
from that is born the sun until it sets.
(from whence the sun is born until it sets.)

kantɛn ɛn su kapiʎa
¡Canten en su capilla
Let them sing in their choir

ɛŋ gɾam maɾaβiʎa
en gran maravilla!
in great wonder!

a kɔn su βɔz muj iŋgɾata iŋgɾata
Ah, con su voz muy ingrata, ingrata,
Ah! With its voice very ungrateful, ungrateful,

akɛl arrɔjwɛlɔ kapɔn dɛ plata
aquel arroyuelo capón de plata,
that small brook gilded of silver,

a la
Ah! La!
Ah! La!

Idiomatic translation:
And may I die of my love for Perinarda. From daybreak to sunset,
let the birds sing and let the branches sound. Let the little birds,
winged sopranos, sing sweetly in their gentle chorus. And may I die
of love for Perinarda. From daybreak to sunset, let them sing in their
choir in great wonder! Ah, and the little brook, gilded with silver,
will add its ungrateful voice. Ah! La!

finɔ kɾistal
Fino cristal (1935)   1:30
Fine Crystal

For Conchita Badía
Carlos Rodriguez Pintos, poet

Vocal Range: C^4 to F^5
For voice and piano

    "Fino cristal," one of Maestro Rodrigo's earliest songs, is
dedicated to Conchita Badía, a well-known soprano and friend of the
composer.[15]

finɔ kɾistal mi niɲɔ
Fino cristal, mi niño,
Fine crystal, my boy child,

finɔ kɾistal
fino cristal,
fine crystal,

palɔmitɾaz ðɛl ajɾɛ
palomitras del aire
little doves of the air

βjɛnɛn i βan
vienen y van.
they come and they go.

rɛðɔndɔ ɛl sɔl rɛðɔndɔ
Redondo el sol redondo
Round the sun round

βaxɔ ɛl pinar
bajo el pinar,
it descends the pines,

lixɛɾɔ ɛl βjɛntɔ nɛɣɾɔ
ligero, el viento negro
agile the wind black
(light and agile the black wind)

kɔrrɛ ðɛtɾas
corre detrás.
passes behind.

aj kɛ aj dɛ mi niɲɔ
Ay que ay, de mi niño
Oh! Oh, of my child

sɔβɾɛ la mar
sobre la mar...
on the sea...

ɛntɾɛ laz nuβɛz βlaŋkas
entre las nubes blancas,
between the clouds white,
(between the white clouds,)

finɔ kɾistal
fino cristal...
fine crystal...

Idiomatic translation:
Fine crystal, my little boy, fine crystal. The little doves fly here and there. As the sun shines, the dark winds sweep through the pines. Oh, my child, there on the sea, between the white clouds. Fine crystal.

fɔljas kanaɾjas
Folías Canarias (1958)   2:30
Song from the Canary Islands

To Sophíe Noël
Anonymous poet

Vocal range: G^4 to E^5
For voice and guitar

Sophíe Noël, a soprano and friend of Sephardic origin, preferred to sing with guitar accompaniment, so this song was a favorite of hers. As "jota" is the typical dance rhythm of Aragon, "folías" is the generic name of the popular folk rhythms of the Canary Islands.[16]

gɾaŋ kanaɾja sɛ a ðɔrmiðɔ
Gran Canaria se ha dormido
Grand Canary has fallen asleep

kɔn ɛl arruʎɔ ðɛl mar
con el arrullo del mar
with the cooing of the sea

nɔ la ðɛspjɛrtɛs izlɛɲa
no la despiertes isleña
not her awaken, island woman
(do not awaken her, island woman)

dɛxa la a undɛskansar
deja la a undescansar
still let her slumber

gɾaŋ kanaɾja sɛ a ðɔrmiðɔ
Gran Canaria se a dormido
Grand Canary has fallen asleep

kɔn ɛl arruʎɔ ðɛl mar
con el arrullo del mar.
with the cooing of the sea.

Idiomatic translation:
   The Canaries have fallen asleep listening to the cooing of the sea.
Don't awaken her, island woman, but let her slumber.

pɔr majɔ ɛɾa pɔr majɔ
Por mayo, era por mayo (1960)   2:55
In May it was, in May

Anonymous poet
Vocal Range: E^4 to A^5

For voice and piano

   This song is also called "Romancillo" in some editions. It is
dedicated to Consuelo Rubio, an excellent soprano, who was accompanied frequently by Maestro Rodrigo.[17]

pɔr majɔ ɛɾa pɔr majɔ
Por mayo, era por mayo,
In May, it was in May,

kwandɔ aθɛ la kalɔr
cuando hace la calor,
when it is hot,

kwandɔ lɔs tɾiyɔs sɛŋkaʎan
cuando los trigos se encallan,
when the wheat is growing,

jɛstan lɔs kampɔs ɛɱ flɔr
y están los campos en flor;
and they were the fields in bloom;
(and the countryside is in bloom;)

kwandɔ kanta la kalandɾja
cuando canta la calandria
when sings the lark
(when the lark sings)

i respondɛl rwisɛɲɔr
y responde el ruiseñor
and responds the nightingale
(and the nightingale responds)

kwandɔ lɔs ɛnamɔɾaðɔs
cuando los enamorados
when the lovers

ban a sɛrβir al amɔr
van a servir al amor.
go to serve love.

mɛnɔs jɔ tɾistɛ kwitaðɔ
Menos yo, ¡triste cuitado!
Except I, sad worried!

kɛ βiβɔ ɛn ɛsta pɾisjɔn
que vivo en esta prisión,
that I live in this prison,

kɛ nɔ sɛ kwandɔ ɛz ðɛ ðia
que no sé cuándo es de día
that not I know when is the day
(that I do not know when it is day)

ni kwandɔ laz nɔtʃɛs sɔn
ni cuándo las noches son
nor when the nights are

sinɔ pɔr unaβɛθiʎa
sino por una avecilla
except for a small bird

kɛ mɛ kantaβal alβɔr
que me cantaba al albor.
that to me it sang at dawn.
(that sang to me at dawn.)

matɔmɛla um baʎɛstɛɾɔ
Matómela un ballestero
Killed it for me an archer
(an archer killed it)

djɔz lɛ ðɛ mal ɣalarðɔn
Dios le dé mal galardón!
God him give evil prize!
(God give him evil prize!)

Idiomatic translation:
It was in May, when the days are hot, the wheat is growing and the countryside is in bloom. It was then that the lark sings, the nightingale responds, and the lovers go to enjoy love. But worried me, I live in a prison. I don't know when it is day or night except for a little bird who sang to me at dawn. An archer killed it. God will reward his mistake!

pɾimaβɛɾa
Primavera (1950)   5:15
Spring

Guillermo Fernández Shaw, poet
Vocal Range: E^4 to D^6

For light soprano, piano, and flute

naθɛn aβɛs i flɔɾɛs
Nacen aves y flores
They are born birds and flowers
(Birds and flowers are born)

i lɔs ajɾɛs sɛ ʎɛnan dɛ tɾinɔs jaɾɔmas
y los aires se llenan de trinos y aromas
and the air itself fills of warbles and perfumes
(and the air is filled with warbles and perfumes)

ɛn la tarðɛ ðɛ amɔr i paθ a dɛ mil kɔlɔɾɛs
en la tarde de amor y paz, ah, de mil colores.
in the afternoon of love and peace of thousand colors.

tɔ̆ŏ tjɛmbɫaj palpita baxɔ un θjɛlɔ ŏɛ nakar
Todo tiembla y palpita bajo un cielo de nácar
All trembles and throbs under a sky of mother-of-pearl.

kɛ βɾiʎa ɣɔθɔsɔ kɔn latiŏɔz ŏɛ luz ŏɛl sɔl
que brilla gozoso con latidos de luz del sol
that sparkles delighted with throbbings from light of the sun

i kɔŋ kanθjɔnɛs
y con canciones.
and with songs.

mwɛɾɛ tiβja la tarŏɛ
Muere tibia la tarde,
It dies warmly in the afternoon,

jɛn la rama ŏɛ un tilɔ
y en la rama de un tilo
and in the branch of a linden tree

ŏɛsyɾana su kantɔ
desgrana su canto
lose their song

rwisɛɲɔɾɛs kɛ tɾinan
ruiseñores que trinan
nightingales that warble

al sɔl dɔɾaŏɔ
al sol dorado.
to the sun golden.
(to the golden sun.)

paxaɾiʎɔs kɛ kɾuθan ɛl ɛŋkaxɛ ŏɛ ɔɾɔ
Pajarillos que cruzan el encaje de oro
Little birds that cross the lace of gold

salpikaŏɔ ŏɛ aθul dɛl tɾamɔntɔ sɔlar
salpicado de azul, del tramonto solar
splashed of blue, it sings behind the mountains sun's rays

kɔn sus plumas pintaðas
con sus plumas pintadas
with their plumes painted

ɛn un raptɔ ðɛ amɔr
en un rapto de amor
in a rapture of love

sɛan lanθaðɔ a βɔlar
se han lanzado a volar
themselves they have determined to fly

si palpitaz ðɛ amɔr
¡Si palpitas de amor
If you beat from love

paxaɾiʎɔ ðɛ aβɾil
pajarillo de abril
little bird of April

nɔ tɛ impɔrtɛ sɛr flɔr
no te importe ser flor!
not you care about being a flower!
(you won't want to be a flower!)

tɔðɔ tjɛmblaj palpita
Todo tiembla y palpita
All trembles and throbs

βaxɔ un θjɛlɔ dɛ nakar
bajo un cielo de nácar
under a sky of mother-of-pearl

kɛ bɾiʎa yɔθɔsɔ
que brilla gozoso
that sparkles delighted

kɔn latiðɔz ðɛ luθ ðɛl sɔl
con latidos de luz del sol
with throbbings of the light of the sun

i kɔŋ kanθjɔnɛs
y con canciones.
and with songs.

la luz ðɛl sɔl sɛ βa
La luz del sol se va
The light from the sun itself goes
(The sun's light goes)

ɛm bɾaθɔz ðɛl amɔr
en brazos del amor.
in arms of love.

naθɛn aβɛs i flɔɾɛs
Nacen aves y flores
They are born birds and flowers
(Birds and flowers are born)

ɛn la tarðɛ kɛ mwɛɾɛ
en la tarde que muere
in the afternoon that dies

jaʎa lɔ lɛxɔs
y allá a lo lejos,
and there in the distance,

kantandɔ kɛða
cantando queda
sung tranquil

la βɔz ðɛl aɣwa
la voz del agua.
the voice of water.

Idiomatic translation:
    In the spring, birds and flowers are born, and they fill the air with warbles and perfumes. The afternoon is one of love, peace, and a thousand colors. All trembles and throbs under a mother-of-pearl sky that sparkles, delighted with the throbbings and songs from the light of the sun. The sounds and aromas die in the afternoon, and in the branch of a linden tree, the warbling nightingales sing to the golden sun. The little birds are determined to fly across the lace of gold sprinkled with blue as the sun's rays sink behind the mountains

in a rapture of love. Because you can beat your wings with love, little bird of April, you won't want to be a flower! All trembles and throbs under a sky of mother-of-pearl that sparkles delighted with the throbbings of the light from the sun and with songs. The light of the sun disappears into the arms of love. In the spring, birds and flowers are born in the afternoon that dies, and there in the distance, the water has sung tranquilly.

rɔmanθɛ ðɛ ðuɾandartɛ

Romance de Durandarte (1955)   4:00

Ballad of Durandarte

Anonymous text--adapted by Victoria Kamhi

Vocal Range: E^4 to F^5

For voice and guitar

"Romance de Durandarte" is one of the ballads from Rodrigo's ballet, *Pavana real*, which takes place in the fifteenth and sixteenth centuries at the court of Germana de Foix in Valencia. The plot describes the life and customs of the vihuelists of the time, in particular Luis de Milán.[18]

duɾandartɛ duɾandartɛ

Durandarte, Durandarte

Durandarte, Durandarte

bwɛŋ kaβaʎɛɾɔ pɾɔβaðɔ

buen caballero probado

good knight proven

(you have proven to be a good knight)

aj

¡ay!

ah!

akɔrðartɛ ðɛβɛɾias

Acordarte deberías

You should remember

dakɛl βwɛn tjɛmpɔ pasaðɔ
D'aquel buen tiempo pasado,
Of that good time passed,

aj
¡ay!
ah!

kwandɔ ɛŋ galas i kanθjɔnɛs
Cuando en galas y canciones
when in galas and songs

puβlikaβas tu kwiðaðɔ
publicabas tu cuidado,
you revealed your care,

aj
¡ay!
ah!

ayɔɾa dɛskɔnɔθiðɔ
Agora, desconocido,
Now unknown,

di pɔr kɛ mɛ as ɔlβiðaðɔ
dí por qué me has olvidado,
tell for why me has forgotten,
(tell me why you have forgotten me,)

aj
¡ay!
ah!

pwɛs amastɛjs a ɣajfɛɾas
Pues, amásteis a Gaiferas
Thus, you loved Gaiferas

kwandɔ jɔ fwi ðɛstɛrraðɔ
cuando yo fui desterrado,
when I was banished,

aj
¡ay!
ah!

i pɔr nɔ sufɾir ultɾaxɛ
Y por no sufrir ultraje,
and to not suffer outrage,
(and not for suffering outrage,)

mɔɾiɾɛ ðɛsɛspɛɾaðɔ
moriré desesperado.
I will die in despair.

aj
¡ay!
ah!

Idiomatic translation:
Good knight, remember how you used to love me? In your songs, you revealed your love for me. For an unknown reason, you have forgotten me. You fell in love with Gaiferas while I was gone. I will not die of outrage, but of despair.

rɔmanθɛ ðɛl kɔmɛndaðɔr ðɛ ɔkaɲa
Romance del Comendador de Ocaña (1948)　　　5:20
Ballad of the Knight Commander of Ocaña

For Lola Rodriguez de Aragón
Lope de Vega, poet--adapted liberally by Joaquín de Entrambasaguas

Vocal Range: C#4 to B5

For voice and piano or voice and orchestra

This song is dedicated to Lola Rodriguez de Aragón, the godmother of Cecilia Rodrigo and one of the Maestro's closest friends. She premiered this setting of Vega's famous, classic epic. Originally for voice and orchestra, *Romance del Comendador de Ocaña* has not yet been published in that form. It will be released in its original version in the fall of 1999.[19]

The text is taken from the historical drama, *Peribáñez y el Comendador de Ocaña*, written between 1605 and 1613. The chief characters include a villainous nobleman, the commoner Peribáñez, and the king who defends him. In this "honor play," themes of Spanish dignity and resistance to oppression are prominent. Also typical is the presentation of an honest, innocent peasant woman who is viewed as prey by the evil aristocrat. In the end, Peribáñez saves the honor of his wife, Casilda, kills the offender, and his actions are approved by the king.[20]

In this passage, Casilda is reprimanding the Comendador who, after sending Peribáñez on a trip so that Casilda is unprotected, has stolen into her house in the middle of the night to seduce her. She mocks the Comendador, saying that he should have a highborn lady with fine clothes and a rich carriage, not a poor peasant girl.

mas kjɛɾɔ jɔ a pɛɾiβaɲɛθ
Más quiero yo a Peribáñez
More love I to Peribáñez
(I love Peribáñez more)

kɔn su kapa la parðiʎa
con su capa la pardilla
with his cloak the peasant
(with his peasant's cloak)

kɛ al kɔmɛndaðɔr ðɛ ɔkaɲa
que al Comendador de Ocaña
than the Commander of Ocaña

kɔn la suja ɣwarnɛθiða
con la suya guarnecida.
with it his garnished one.
(with his garnished one.)

la muxɛr ðɛ pɛɾiβaɲɛθ
La mujer de Peribáñez
The wife of Peribáñez

la maz βɛʎa ɛz ðɛ la βiʎa
la más bella es de la villa
the most beautiful she is of the small town
(is the most beautiful woman of the village)

jɛl kɔmɛndaðɔr ðɛ ɔkaɲa
y el Comendador de Ocanã
and the Commander of Ocaña

ðɛ amɔɾɛz la rɛkɛɾia
de amores la requería.
for loves her he would require.
(for love he would require her.)

la muxɛr ɛz βirtuɔsa
La mujer es virtuosa
The woman is virtuous

kwantɔ ɛrmɔsaj kwantɔ linda
cuanto hermosa y cuanto linda;
so beautiful and so pretty;

mjɛntras su ɛspɔsɔ ɛstausɛntɛ
mientras su esposo está ausente
while her husband is absent

ðɛsta swɛrtɛ rɛspɔndia
de esta suerte respondía;
from this luck he responded; (the commander)

sɛyaðɔr kɛ ðɛzðɛ lɛxɔs
Segador que desde lejos
Harvester that from faraway
(harvester who is from far away)

az βɛniðɔ a nwɛstra βiʎa
has venido a nuestra villa
you have come to our small town

kɔnβiðaðɔ ðɛl ayɔstɔ
convidado del agosto
dinner guest of August

kjɛn tɛ ðjɔ tanta maliθja
¿quién te dió tanta malicia?
who you gave so much malice?

kwandɔ salʸan las ɛstɾ̞ɛʎas
Cuando salgan las estrellas
When they leave the stars
(when the stars leave)

a tu ðɛskansɔ kamina
a tu descanso camina,
to your rest walk,
(walk to your rest,)

i nɔ tɛ mɛtas ɛŋ kɔsaz
y no te metas en cosas
and not you get into in things
(and do not get into things)

ðɛ kɛ alʸun sɛ tɛ siʸa
de que algún se te siga.
of which one you follow.
(of which one may follow you.)

kjɛɾɔ mɛxɔr βɛr mi ðwɛɲɔ
Quiero mejor ver mi dueño
I wish best to see my master
(I want most to see my master)

ɛn su xaka la tɔrðiʎa
en su jaca la tordilla,
on his pony the dapple-grey
(on his dapple-grey pony)

ʎɛna ðɛskartʃa la βarβa
llena de escarcha la barba
full of frost the beard
(his beard full of frost)

i ðɛ njɛβɛ la kamisa
y de nieve la camisa.
and of snow the shirt.
(and snow on his shirt.)

la βaʎa ɛstatɾaβɛsaða
La balla está atravesada
The crossbow goes through (crosses)

jamarraðɔs a la siʎa
y amarrados a la silla
and fastens to the seat,

ðɔs pɛrðiθɛs ɔ kɔnɛxɔs
dos perdices o conejos
two partridges or rabbits

jɛl pɔðɛŋkɔ ðɛ trajʎa
y el podenco de trailla,
and the hound of leash,
(and the leashed hound,)

kɛ βɛr al kɔmɛndaðɔr
que ver al Comendador
than to see the Commander

kɔŋ γaβan dɛ sɛða rika
con gabán de seda rica,
with overcoat of silk rich,
(with his overcoat of rich silk,)

aðɔrnaðɔz ðɛ ðjamantɛs
adornados de diamantes
adorned of diamonds
(adorned with diamonds)

ɛl xuβɔn i la kapiʎa
el jubón y la capilla,
the doublet and the hood

ðɛ kaθa kɔn suz mɔntɛɾɔs
de caza con sus monteros
for hunting with his huntsmen

kaβalγandɔ ɛn dʒɛγwa fina
cabalgando en yegua fina
riding on a mare fine
(riding on a fine mare)

kɔn ɛl alkɔn ɛn la manɔ
con el halcón en la mano
with the falcon in the hand

jɛl puɲal dɛ ɔɾɔ ɛn la θinta
y el puñal de oro en la cinta.
and the dagger of gold in the belt.

mas kjɛɾɔ jɔ a pɛɾiβaɲɛθ
Más quiero yo a Peribáñez,
More love I Peribáñez,
(I love Peribáñez more,)

kɔn su kapa la parðiʎa
con su capa la pardilla,
with his cloak the peasant
(with his peasant's cloak)

kɛ al kɔmɛndaðɔr ðɛ ɔkaɲa
que al Comendador de Ocaña
than the Commander of Ocaña

kɔn la suja ɣwarnɛθiða
con la suya guarnecida.
with his garnished one.

ɛl kɔmɛndaðɔr ðɛ okaɲa
El Comendador de Ocaña
The Commander of Ocaña

sɛrβiɾa ðama ðɛstimanɔ
servirá a dama de estimano
he will serve to the mistress of estime
(the type of dress worn in Leon)

kɔn sajwɛlɔ ðɛ ɣɾana
con sayuelo de grana
with wearing the little dress of scarlet

ni sarta ðɛ arxɛntɛɾia
ni sarta de argentería.
nor string of gold embroidery.
(She wears the dress of the poor, not clothing of gold embroidery.)

lɛaβlaɾa ɛn diskɾɛtas kartaz
Le hablará en discretas cartas
She will speak in discreet letters

ðɛ su amɔr a maɾaβiʎa
de su amor a maravilla,
of her love wondrous,
(of her wondrous love,)

nɔ kampɛsinɔz ðɛzðɛnɛs
no campesinos desdenes,
no countrymen disdains,
(no disdainful countrymen,)

ɛnβwɛltɔs ɛn sɛɲɔɾia
envueltos en señoría.
wrapped up in lordship.

ʎɛɣaɾa ɛŋ xɛntil karrɔθa
Llegará en gentil carroza
She will arrive in charming carriage

lɔz ðisantɔs a la misa
los disantos a la misa,
the   holy days to the mass,
(to mass on holy days,)

nɔ βɛndɾa ɛŋ karrɔ ðɛstakaz
no vendrá en carro, de estacas
not she will come in cart, of sticks
(she will not arrive in a poor cart)

ðɛ lɔs kampɔs a laz βiɲas
de los campos a las viñas.
of the countrysides and the vineyards.

ɔlɛɾalɛ a ɣwantɛz ðɛ ambar
Olerále a guantes de ambar,
It will smell to gloves of amber,
(Her gloves will smell of amber,)

a pɛrfumɛs i pastiʎas
a perfumes y pastillas,
of perfumes and soap,

nɔ a tɔmiʎɔ ni a kantwɛsɔ
no a tomillo ni a cantueso,
not of thyme nor of lavender,

mɛntas i θarθas flɔɾiðas
mentas y zarzas floridas.
peppermint and brambles flowering.

bɛtɛ pwɛs ɛl sɛɣaðɔr
Vete, pues, el segador,
You leave, then, harvester,

mala fwɛɾɛ la tu ðitʃa
mala fuere la tu dicha,
it would be bad, as you say,

kɛ si pɛɾiβaɲɛz βjɛnɛ
que si Peribáñez viene,
that if Peribáñez comes,

nɔ βɛɾaz la luz ðɛl ðia
no verás la luz del día.
not you will see the light of the day.
(you will not see the light of day.)

jaun kwandɔ ɛl kɔmɛndaðɔr
Y aún cuando el Comendador
And yet when the Commander

mɛ amaɾɛ kɔmɔ a su βiða
me amare como a su vida
to me he should love as he loves his life
(should love me as he loves his life)

i sɛ ŏjɛsɛŋ fama jɔnɾa
y se diesen fama y honra
and they give him fame and honor

pɔr amɔɾɔsaz mɛntiɾas
por amorosas mentiras.
for loving deceitfulness.

mas kjɛɾɔ jɔ a pɛɾiβaɲɛθ
Más quiero yo a Peribáñez
More love I to Peribáñez
(I love Peribáñez more)

kɔn su kapa la parŏiʎa
con su capa la pardilla
with his cloak the peasant
(with his peasant's cloak)

kɛ al kɔmɛndaŏɔr ŏɛ ɔkaɲa
que al Comendador de Ocaña
than the Commander of Ocaña

kɔn la suja ɣwarnɛθiŏa
con la suya guarnecida. ¡Ah!
with his garnished one. Ah!

Idiomatic translation:
I love the peasant Peribáñez more with his peasant's cloak than the Commander of Ocaña with all his fine clothes.

Peribáñez's wife is the most beautiful of all, and the Commander of Ocaña wanted her. But she is virtuous and so beautiful that while her husband was away, the Commander decided to try to win her.

Reaper (Commander), you have come to our villa as an August dinner guest. Who gave you so much hate? When dawn comes, walk until you find a place to rest and don't get into trouble, or your trouble may come to haunt you. I want to see my love on his dapple-gray pony, with his beard full of frost and snow on his shirt. I want to see his crossbow fastened to his seat and two partridges or rabbits and his hound running beside him. I would rather see him than the Commander with his rich silk coat adorned with diamonds. I would rather see my love than the Commander riding on a fine mare with a falcon in his hand and a gold dagger in his belt. I love Peribáñez more with his peasant's coat than the Commander of Ocaña with all his fine

clothes. Why would the Commander prefer to serve a mistress of Leon in her plain dress without gold or scarlet embroidery? He should speak in discreet letters of his wondrous love, not to disdainful countrymen. He should have a fine lady who will arrive at mass in a charming carriage, not in a poor cart. Her amber gloves will smell of perfume, not of thyme, lavender, peppermint, or brambles. You leave, Commander, or things will be bad for you, because if Peribáñez comes, you will not live to see the light of day. And when the Commander loves me as much as he loves his own life, he will be honored and famous for his deceitfulness. Besides, I love Peribáñez more with his peasant's cloak than the Commander of Ocaña with his fine clothes. Ah!

sɔβæl kupɛj
Sobre el Cupey (1965)   1:50
On the Cupey
(A cupey is a small tree with white flowers that grows in the Carribean.)

For Maria Esther Robles
Luis Hernandez Aquino, poet
Vocal Range: D^4 to E^b
For voice and piano

A Puerto Rican Christmas Carol

Victoria and Joaquín Rodrigo traveled to Puerto Rico in August 1963, so that Maestro Rodrigo could teach a two-semester course on the History of Music at the University of Puerto Rico in Rio Piedras. The poet was a professor at the university at the time.[21]

The Puerto Rican soprano Maria Esther Robles, to whom this song is dedicated, became a friend of the Rodrigos during their stay in Puerto Rico.[22]

palɔmikaz ðɛ ɔɾɔ
Palomicas de oro
Little doves of gold

ɛn ɛl tʃinar
en el chinar,
in the pebbles,

kjɛβɾan ɛl ajɾɛ kjetɔ
quiebran el aire quieto
break the air still
(break the still air)

kɔn su kantar
con su cantar.
with their song.

ba la βirxɛn tɛndjɛndɔ
Va la Virgen tendiendo
She goes the Virgin laying out
(the Virgin spreads out)

sɔβɾɛl kupɛj
sobre el cupey
on the cupey

lɔs paɲalɛz ðiβinɔz
los pañales divinos
the swaddling cloths divine
(the divine swaddling cloths)

ðɛl niɲɔ rɛi
del Niño Rey.
of the Child King.

dwɛrmɛl niɲɔ su swɛɲɔ
Duerme el Niño su sueño,
Sleep the Child his dream,
(the Child sleeps his dream,)

kanta ɛl kɔki
canta el coquí.
sings the coqui.
(the coqui sings.)
(A frog, the coqui, is the adopted national animal in Puerto Rico.)

i la tarðɛ sɛ tiɲɛ
y la tarde se tiñe
and the afternoon is dyed

ðɛ ambar jaɲil
de ambar y añil.
of amber and indigo.

asi kanta la βirxɛn
Así canta la Virgen
So sings the Virgin

kɔm boθ ðɛl mjɛl
con voz de miel;
with voice of honey;

dwɛrmɛ sɔl dɛ mi alma
"¡Duerme, sol de mi alma
"Sleep, sun of my soul

flɔr ðɛ jsɾæl
flor de Israel!" Ah.
flower of Israel!" Ah.

Idiomatic translation:
    Little gold doves in the pebbles sing in the still air. The Virgin spreads the swaddling clothes of the Child King on the cupey. As the Child dreams his dreams, the coqui sings in the amber and indigo afternoon. The Virgin sings with a voice of honey, "Sleep, sun of my soul, flower of Israel!" Ah!

sɔnɛtɔ
Soneto (1934)   2:45
Sonnet

To Victoria de los Angeles
Juan Bautista de Mesa, poet

Vocal Range: C#^{4} to A^5
For voice and piano

    As stated earlier, the Rodrigos enjoyed a friendly relationship with Victoria de los Angeles. They had attended her debut at the Cultural Society of Madrid when she was only twenty years old, in March 1945. Vicky said of that concert:

She sang two of Joaquín's songs: "Serranilla" and "Coplas del Pastor Enamorado," with a purity of style and diction, and a sensitivity that left us enthralled. And what a voice she had! That twenty-year-old girl was already a diva![23]

dɔrmia ɛn um pɾaðɔ mi pastɔɾa ɛrmɔsa
Dormía en un prado mi pastora hermosa,
Slept in a meadow my shepherdess pretty,
(My pretty shepherdess was sleeping in a meadow,)

jɛn tɔrnɔ ðɛʎa ɛrraβa ɛntɾɛ las flɔɾɛs
y en torno della erraba, entre las flores,
and in I wandered about her, among the flowers,

dɛ unaj ɔtɾa usurpandɔ lɔz likɔɾɛs
de una y otra usurpando los licores,
from one and other usurping the liqueurs,

unaβɛxwɛla mas kɛ jɔ ðitʃɔsa
una abejuela, más que yo dichosa,
a bee, more than I happy,
(a bee, happier than I,)

kɛ βjɔ lɔz laβjɔs dɔndɛ amɔr rɛpɔsa
que vió los labios donde amor reposa,
that he saw the lips where love rested,

ja kjɛn ɛl alβa ɛmbia sus kɔlɔɾɛs
y a quién el alba envía sus colores,
and to whom the dawn sends her colors,

kɛ al βwɛlɔ rɛfɾɛnandɔ lɔs ɛrrɔɾɛs
que al vuelo refrenando los errores,
that to the flight holding back the errors,

ɛŋgaɲaða lɔz mwɛrðɛ kɔmɔ a rɔsa
engañada, los muerde como a rosa.
deceived, them he bit like a rose.
(he bit the lips like a rose.)

ɔ βɛnturɔsɔ ɛrrɔr diskɾɛtɔ ɛŋgaɲɔ
¡Oh venturoso error, discreto engaño!
Oh, lucky error, discreet deceit!

ɔ tɛmɛɾaɾjaβɛxa pwɛs tɔkastɛ
¡Oh, temeraria abeja, pues tocaste
Oh, rash bee, then you touched

dɔndɛ aun imaxinarlɔ nɔ mɛ atɾɛβɔ
donde aún imaginarlo no me atrevo!
where to imagine it not to me dare!
(I would not dare!)

si as sɛntiðɔ ðɛmbiðja ɛl tristɛ ðaɲɔ
Si has sentido de envidia el triste daño
If you have felt of envy the sad damage

partɛ kɔmmiyɔ ɛl nɛktar kɛ rɔβastɛ
parte conmigo el néctar que robaste,
leave with me the nectar that you robbed,

tɛ ðɛβɛɾɛ lɔ kɛ al amɔr nɔ ðɛβɔ
te deberé lo que al amor no debo...
you I will owe that the love not I owe...
(I will be indebted to you that which to love I do not owe.)

Idiomatic translation:
    My pretty shepherdess was sleeping in a meadow and I wandered
around her, among the flowers. A bee, happier than I, went also from
flower to flower, drawing nectar. It saw her lips, where love rested and
to whom the dawn sends her colors and, making a mistake, bit her
lips pretending they were a rose. Oh, lucky error, shrewd deception!
The rash bee touched where I only imagine touching. I couldn't dare!
If you have felt envy because of your mistake, give me the nectar you
robbed. I will be indebted to you even though I am not indebted to
love.

un ɔmɛ san antɔnjɔ
¡Un Home, San Antonio!   2:49
A Man, Saint Antonio!

For Antonio Fernández Cid
Rosalía de Castro, poet
Vocal Range: C^4 to A^5
For voice and piano

"¡Un Home, San Antonio!" was commissioned by Orense, an important city in Galicia, as a tribute to Antonio Fernández Cid. Cid, originally from Galicia, was a famous music critic in Madrid. Rodrigo selected this text, by the Galician poet, Rosalía de Castro.[24] Her brief biography is stated with *Rosaliana*, a song cycle setting four of her poems.

san antɔnjɔ βɛnditɔ
San Antonio bendito,
San Antonio blessed,
(Blessed San Antonio,)

daðɛmɛ un ɔmɛ
dádeme un home,
give me a man,

san antɔnjɔ βɛnditɔ
San Antonio bendito,
San Antonio blessed,
(Blessed San Antonio,)

aŋkɛ mɛ matɛ
anque me mate,
even if me he mistreats,

aŋkɛ mɛsfɔlɛ
anque me esfole.
even if me he dishonors.
(even if he dishonors me.)

mɛu santɔ san antɔnjɔ
Meu Santo San Antonio,
Please Saint San Antonio,

dajmɛ un ɔmiɲɔ
daime un homiño,
give me a little man,

dajmɛ un ɔmiɲɔ
daime un homiño,
give me a little man,

aŋkɔ tamaɲɔ tɛɲa
anqu'ó tamaño teña
although if he might have
(although he might be no bigger than)

dun ɣɾan dɛ miʎɔ
d'un gran de millo.
a grain of millet.

dajmɔ mɛu santɔ
Daimo, meu Santo
Give me, please Saint

aŋkɔs pɛs taɲa kɔʃɔs
anqu'os pés taña coxos,
although his feet may be crippled

maŋkɔs ɔz βɾaθɔs
mancos os brazos.
maimed his arms.

una muʎɛr sin ɔmɛ
Una muller sin home...
A wife without a man...

santɔ βɛnditɔ
¡Santo bendito!
Saint blessed!

ɛ kɔrpiɲɔ sin alma
E corpiño sin alma,
Is a body without a soul,

fɛsta sin tɾiɣɔ
festa sin trigo.
a fiesta without bread.

pau βiɾaðɔjɾɔ
Pau viradoiro,
Post spinning,

a
¡Ah!
Ah!

kɔnda kɛjɾa kɛ βaja
qu'onda queira que vaya,
that wherever it goes,

tɾɔntʃɔ kɛ tɾɔntʃɔ
troncho que troncho
cut that cuts
(cutting here and there)

majs ɛntɛndun ɔmiɲɔ
Mais enten'un homiño
But having a man

biʃɛ ðɔ karmɛ
¡Vixe do Carme!
Virgin of Carmen!

nɔn aj mundɔ kɛ tʃɛɣɛ
Non hay mundo que chegue
Not enough world that covers
(the world will not hold)

paɾa un fɔlɣarsɛ
para un folgarse.
for a joy.
(my joy.)

kɛ θambɛu tɾɛŋkɔ
¡Que zamb'eu trenco,
Even if he is knock-kneed,

sɛmpɾɛ βɔ tɛr un ɔmɛ
sempre é bó ter un home
always is having a man
(to have a man)

paɾa un rɛmɛǒjɔ
para un remedio!
for a remedy!
(is always the solution!)

san antɔnjɔ βɛnditɔ
¡San Antonio bendito!
Saint Antonio blessed!

daǒɛmɛ un ɔmɛ
¡dademe un home!
give me a man!

Idiomatic translation:
Blessed Saint Antonio, give me a man. Even if he kills me or dishonors me, please Saint Antonio, give me a little man. Although he may be no bigger than a grain of millet, please give him to me, Saint. Although his feet may be crippled or he may be armless, please give him to me. A woman without a man, blessed Saint, is a body without a soul, a fiesta without bread. A woman without a man is a useless spinning post, ah, that wherever it goes, cutting here and there to no avail. But having a man, Virgin of Carmen, if one has a man, there is no end to joy! Even if he is knock-kneed, to have a man is the remedy. Blessed Saint Antonio, give me a man.

Notes

1. Victoria Kamhi, *Hand in Hand with Joaquín Rodrigo, My Life at the Maestro's Side,* trans. Ellen Wilkerson (Pittsburgh: Latin American Literary Review Press, 1992), 226-227.
2. Cecilia Rodrigo, interview with author, July 24, 1998.
3. Kamhi, *Hand in Hand,* 112.
4. Kamhi, *Hand in Hand,* 140.
5. C. Rodrigo, interview, July 24, 1998.
6. Kamhi, *Hand in Hand,* 94.
7. Kamhi, *Hand in Hand,* 106.
8. Philip Ward, ed., The Oxford *Companion to Spanish Literature* (Oxford: Clarendon Press, 1978), 307.
9. C. Rodrigo, interview, July 24, 1998.
10. Ward, *Oxford Companion,* 597.
11. C. Rodrigo, interview, July 24, 1998.
12. Ward, *Oxford Companion,* 212.

13. Ward, *Oxford Companion*, 470.
14. C. Rodrigo, E-mail, November 16, 1998.
15. C. Rodrigo, E-mail, October 5, 1998.
16. C. Rodrigo, E-mail, October 5, 1998.
17. C. Rodrigo, E-mail, April 23, 1998.
18. C. Rodrigo, E-mail, October 5, 1998.
19. Rodrigo, interview, July 24, 1998.
20. Dian Fox, *Refiguring the Hero* (University Park: The Pennsylvania State University Press), 101.
21. Kamhi, *Hand in Hand*, 211.
22. C. Rodrigo, E-mail, November 16, 1998.
23. Kamhi, *Hand in Hand*, 130.
24. C. Rodrigo, E-mail, October 5, 1998.

Chapter 4

Canciones de dos épocas

kanθjɔnɛz ŏɛ ŏɔs ɛpɔkas

Canciones de dos épocas   12:35
Songs of Two Epochs
    Cantiga (1925)--Gil Vicente (1465?-1536?)   2:40
    Romance de la infantina de Francia (1928)--anon.   5:15
    Serranilla (1928)--Marqués de Santillana (1398-1458) 2:00
    Árbol (1987)--Fina de Calderón   1:15
    ¿Por qué te llamaré? (1987)--Fina de Calderón   1:25

Vocal Range: C^4 to A^5
For voice and piano

This cycle is particularly interesting because of the variety of the poetry, dating from the fifteenth century to the twentieth. Also, the first three songs are some of Rodrigo's early song settings, whereas the last two are among his last composed works.

kantiɣa
1. **Cantiga** (1925)
Ballad

Gil Vicente (1465?-1536?), born in the Portuguese countryside, was a major Portuguese and Spanish-language playwright. Because he was an excellent goldsmith by trade, he was brought to the Évora court in 1490 for the wedding of the Crown Prince of Portugal to Isabel, the daughter of the Catholic Monarchs, Ferdinand and Isabel. There, he directed theatrical events, acted, and wrote both sacred and secular plays. Forty-four of his plays survive, of which sixteen are in Portuguese, eleven in Spanish and the remainder are bilingual. He is acclaimed as the most expressive representative of the dying medieval Portuguese dramatic tradition but also as the founder of the Renaissance style in Portugal.[1]

In the Schott edition, the second tempo marking should be the eighth note = 88, not the quarter note = 88.

muj γɾaθjɔsa ɛz la ðɔnθɛʎa
Muy graciosa es la doncella.
Very graceful is the maiden.

diɣas tu ɛl kaβaʎɛɾɔ
Digas tú el caballero
Tell me, you the knight
(Tell me, knight)

kɛ las armaz βɛstias
que las armas vestias
that the weapons were adorned
(you who are adorned with weapons)

sjɛl kɔβaʎɔ ɔ las armas
si el caballo o las armas
if the horse or the weapons

ɔ la γɛrra ɛs tam bɛʎa
o la guerra es tan bella.
or the war is so beautiful.

diɣas tu ɛl maɾinɛɾɔ
Digas tu el marinero
Tell me, you the sailor
(Tell me, sailor)

kɛn tuz naβɛz βiβias
que en tus naves vivías
that in your ships you lived
(you who live in ships)

si la naβɛ ɔ la βɛla
si la nave o la vela
if the ship or the candle

ɔ la ɛstɾɛʎa ɛs tam bɛʎa
o la estrella es tan bella.
or the star is so beautiful.

diɣas tu ɛl pastɔrθikɔ
Digas tú el pastorcico
Tell me, you the shepherd
(Tell me, shepherd)

kɛl ɣanaðikɔ ɣwarðas
que el ganadico guardas
that the little flock you keep
(you who guard the flock)

sjɛl ɣanaðɔ ɔ lɔz βaʎɛs
si el ganado o los valles
if the flock or the valleys

ɔ la sjɛrra ɛs tam bɛʎa
o la sierra es tan bella
or the mountain is so beautiful.

muj ɣɾaθjɔsa ɛz la ðɔnθɛʎa
Muy graciosa es la doncella.
Very graceful is the maid.

Idiomatic translation:
    The maiden is very graceful. Tell me, knight, you who carry arms, if the horse or the weapons or the war is so beautiful. Tell me, sailor, you who live in ships, if the ship or the candle or the star is so beautiful. Tell me, shepherd, you who guard the flock, if the flock or the valleys or the mountain is so beautiful. The maiden is very graceful.

rɔmanθɛ ðɛ la imɟantina ðɛ fɾanθja

2. **Romance de la infantina de Francia** (1928)
Legend of the little Princess of France

text: anonymous

dɛ fɾanθja partjɔ la niɲa
De Francia partió la niña,
From France she parted the girl,
(From France the little girl parted,)

dɛ fɾanθja la βjɛn ɣwarniða
de Francia la bien guarnida;
from France she well adorned;
(from France, the well-adorned girl;)

iβasɛ paɾa paɾis
íbase para París,
left for Paris,

ðɔ paðɾɛj maðɾɛ tɛnia
do padre y madre tenía:
from father and mother she had:

ɛrraðɔ ʎɛβael kaminɔ
Errado lleva el camino,
Mistaken is the path,

ɛrraðɔ ʎɛβa la ɣia
errada lleva la guía;
mistaken is the guide;

arrimaɾasɛ a un ɾɔβlɛ
arrimárase a un roble,
draw near to the oak,

pɔr ɛspɛɾar kɔmpaɲia
por esperar compañía.
to hope for company.

bjɔ βɛnir a uŋ kaβa𝑓ɛrɔ
Vio venir a un caballero,
She saw come to a knight,
(She saw a knight approach,)

kɛ a parís 𝑓ɛβa la ɣia
que a París lleva la guía.
that to Paris is the guide.
(that is enroute to Paris.)

la niɲa ðɛskɛ lɔ βiðɔ
La niña, desque lo vido,
The girl, upon seeing,

dɛsta swɛrtɛ lɛ ðɛθia
de esta suerte le decía:
of this fate to him she said:
(this fate, she said to him:)

si tɛ plaθɛ kaβa𝑓ɛrɔ
Si te place, caballero,
If you please, knight,

𝑓ɛβɛzmɛn tu kɔmpaɲia
llévesme en tu compañía.
take me in your company.

plaθɛmɛ ðixɔ sɛɲɔra
Pláceme--dijo--señora,
It pleases me, he said, madam,

plaθɛmɛ ðixɔ mi βiða
pláceme--dijo--mi vida.
it pleases me, he said, my life.

apɛɔsɛ ðɛl kaβa𝑓ɔ
Apeóse del caballo
He stepped down from the horse

pɔr aθεʎɛ kɔrtɛsia
por hacelle cortesía;
to give her courtesy;

pusɔ la niɲa ɛn las aŋkas
puso la niña en las ancas
he put the girl on the (horse's) rump

i suβjɛɾasɛn la siʎa
y subiérase en la silla:
and raised her to the saddle:

ɛn ɛl mɛðjɔ ðɛl kaminɔ
en el medio del camino
in the middle of the road

ðɛ amɔɾɛz la rɛkɛɾia
de amores la requería.
of love she was summoned.

la niɲa ðɛskɛ lɔjɛɾa
La niña desque lo oyera
The girl until it could be heard

ðixɔ lɛ kɔn ɔsaðia
díjo le con osadía:
said to him with boldness:

tatɛ tatɛ kaβaʎɛɾɔ
Tate, tate, caballero,
Be careful, careful, knight,

nɔ aɣais tal βiʎania
no hagáis tal villanía:
no taint such a low birth:
(Don't dare to seduce me:)

ixa sɔj ðɛ um malatɔ
hija soy de un malato
daughter I am from a leper
(I am the daughter of a leper)

i ðɛ una malatia
y de una malatía;
and of a female leper;
(and my mother is also a leper;)

ɛl ɔmbɾɛ kɛ a mi ʎɛɣasɛ
el hombre que a mí llegase,
the man who to me comes,

malatɔ sɛ tɔrnaɾia
malato se tornaría.
a leper he will become.

kɔn tɛmɔr ɛl kaβaʎɛɾɔ
Con temor el caballero
With fear the knight

palaβɾa nɔ rɛspɔndia
palabra no respondía.
word not responded.
(could not respond.)

a la ɛntɾaða ðɛ paɾiz
A la entrada de Paris
At the entrance to Paris

la niɲa sɛ sɔnɾɛia
la niña se sonreía,
the girl at him smiled,
(the girl smiled at him,)

dɛ kɛ βɔz rɛis sɛɲɔɾa
¿De qué vos reís, señora?
Of what you laugh, madam?
(Why do you laugh, madam?)

dɛ kɛ βɔz rɛis mi βiða
¿De qué vos reís, mi vida?
Of what you laugh, my life?
(Why do you laugh, my life?)

riɔ mɛ ðɛl kaβaʎɛɾɔ
Río me del caballero,
I laugh to me from the knight,
(I laugh at my knight,)

i ðɛ su ɣɾaŋ kɔβarðia
y de su gran cobardía,
and of his big cowardice,
(and of his grand cowardice,)

tɛnɛr la niɲa ɛn ɛl kampɔ
¡tener la niña en el campo,
To have the girl in the countryside,

i katar lɛ kɔrtɛsia
y catar le cortesía!
and to sample the courtesy!

kɔm bɛɾɣwɛnθa ɛl kaβaʎɛɾɔ
Con vergüenza el caballero
With shame the knight

ɛstas palaβɾaz ðɛθia
estas palabras decia:
these words said:

bwɛlta βwɛlta mi sɛɲɔɾa
–Vuelta, vuelta, mi señora,
Return, return, my lady,

kɛ una kɔsa sɛ mɛ ɔlβiða
que una cosa se me olvida.--
that a thing itself to me I can forget.
(so that I can forget one thing.)

la niɲa kɔmɔ ðiskɾɛta
La niña como discreta
The girl since reasonable (discreet)
(The girl with discretion)

dixɔ jɔ nɔ βɔlβɛɾia
dijo: yo no volvería,
said: I not would go back,
(I would not go back,)

ni pɛrsɔna auŋkɛ βɔl βjɛsɛ
ni persona, aunque vol viese
no one, not even you who sees

ɛm mi kwɛrpɔ tɔkaɾia
en mi cuerpo tocaría:
my body should touch me:

ixa sɔj ðɛl rɛj ðɛ franθja
hija soy del rey de Francia
Girl I am from the king of France
(I am the daughter of the king of France)

i la rɛjna kɔnstantina
y la reina Constantina,
and the queen Constantina,

ɛl ɔmbɾɛ kɛ a mi ʎɛɣasɛ
el hombre que a mí llegase
the man who to me comes

muj kaɾɔ lɛ kɔstaɾia
muy caro le costaría.
much dear the cost.
(will pay dearly.)

Idiomatic translation:
The lovely girl left her mother and father in France and departed for Paris. But she became lost and waited near an oak, hoping that help would soon arrive. Luckily, she saw a knight approach, on his way to Paris. She asked him to take her into his company. With great pleasure, he set the pretty girl on his horse but soon, they began to fall in love and he attempted to seduce her. "Be careful," the girl said. "Don't entangle yourself with me. My parents are lepers and the man who loves me will become a leper, too."
The knight was very afraid and made no response. As they entered Paris, the girl began to laugh. "Why do you laugh, madam? Why do

you laugh, my life?" "I laugh because of your cowardice! In the country, you had the opportunity to seduce me and yet you failed!"

With shame, the knight said,"Return, my dear, and let me forget your story." The girl responded reasonably, "I don't want to go back. No one should ever touch me. I am the daughter of the King of France and the Queen Constantina. The man who loves me will pay dearly."

sɛrraniʎa
3. **Serranilla** (1928)
Rustic Song

Marqués de Santillana (1398-1458), born in Palencia, was a literary critic and poet. When his father died in 1404, he was sent to live with his grandmother, Doña Mencía de Cisneros, a great patroness of art and learning. Because of her influence, he began a vast library, which is now housed at the Biblioteca Nacional in Madrid. Santillana was a man of great learning, fluent in Italian, French, Catalan, and Galician. His poetry is remarkable because it marks the transition from Medieval thought to the Renaissance period. His work is lyrical, often in the troubadour song tradition.[2]

At measure 64, all three staves are in treble clef.

mɔtsa tam fɛrmɔsa
Moça tan fermosa
Young girl so beautiful

nɔn βi ɛn la frɔntɛra
non vi en la frontera,
not I saw in the frontier,
(I did not see in the frontier,)

kɔmɔ una βakɛra
como una vaquera
like a milkmaid

ðɛ la finɔxɔsa
de la Finojosa.
from Finojosa.
(Finojosa is a town in Castilla.)

faθjɛndɔ la βia
Faciendo la via
Making the way
(Traveling)

ðɛl kalatɾaβɛɲɔ
del Calatraveño
from Calatraveño

a santa maɾia
a Santa Maria,
to Santa Maria,

bɛnθiðɔ ðɛl swɛɲɔ
Vencido del sueño,
Conquer by the dream,
(Feeling sleepy,)

pɔr tjɛrra fɾayɔsa
por tierra fragosa
for earth rough
(because of the rough earth)

pɛrðia la karrɛɾa
perdía la carrera,
I lost the race,
(I lost my way,)

dɔ βi la βakɛɾa
do ví la vaquera
I saw the milkmaid
(when I saw the milkmaid)

ðɛ la finɔxɔsa
de la Finojosa.
from the Finojosa.

ɛn um bɛrðɛ pɾaðɔ
En un verde prado
In a green meadow

ðɛ rɔsas ɛ flɔɾɛs
de rosas e flores
of roses and flowers

gwarðandɔ ɣanaðɔ
guardando ganado
guarding cattle

kɔn ɔtɾɔs pastɔɾɛs
con otros pastores,
with other shepherds,

la βi taŋ gɾaθjɔsa
la ví tan graçiosa
she I saw so gracious
(she was so gracious)

kɛ apɛnas kɾɛjɛɾa
que apenas creyera
that hardly I may believe
(that I could hardly believe it)

kɛ fwɛsɛ βakɛɾa
que fuese vaquera
that she was a milkmaid

ðɛ la finɔxɔsa
de la Finojosa.
from the Finojosa.

nɔn kɾɛɔ la rɔsaz
Non creo la rosas
Not I believe the roses
(I do not think the roses)

ðɛ la pɾimaβɛɾa
de la primavera
of the spring

sɛan taŋ fɛrmɔsaz
sean tan fermosas
they may be so beautiful
(could be as beautiful)

nin dɛ tal manɛɾa
nin de tal manera.
by of such manner.
(by any means.)

faβlandɔ siŋ glɔsa
Fablando sin glosa
Speaking without gloss
(If I may speak the truth)

si antɛs supjɛɾa
si antes supiera
if before I had known
(if I had known before)

dɛ akɛʎa βakɛɾa
de aquella vaquera
of that milkmaid

ðɛ la finɔxɔsa
de la Finojosa.
of Finojosa.

nɔn tantɔ miɾaɾa
Non tanto mirara
Not as much I may look
(I could hardly look at)

su mutʃa βɛldað
su mucha beldad,
her much beauty,
(her great beauty,)

pɔrkɛ mɛ ðɛksaɾa
porque me dexara
for that to me left
(because it left me)

ɛm mi liβɛrtað
en mi libertad.
in my liberty.
(free from her.)

maz ðiksɛ ðɔnɔsa
Mas dixe: "Donosa"
But I said: "Charming"

pɔr saβɛr kjɛn ɛɾa
(por saber quien era,
(for I knew who she was,

akɛʎa βakɛɾa
aquella vaquera
that milkmaid

ðɛ la finɔxɔsa
de la Finojosa.)
from Finojosa.)

bjɛŋ kɔmɔ riɛndɔ
Bien como riendo,
Well like laughing,
(As if laughing,)

ðiksɔ βjɛm bɛŋgaðɛs
dixo: "Bien vengades,
she said: "Well, come,

kɛ ja βjɛn ɛntjɛndɔ
que ya bien entiendo
that well I understand
(I already understand)

lɔ kɛ ðɛmandaðɛs
lo que demandades:
it that you demand:
(that which you demand:)

nɔn ɛz ðɛsɛɔsa
non es desseosa
not it is desiring
(it is not a desiring)

ðɛ amar nin lɔ ɛspɛɾa
de amar, nin lo espera,
of love, nor it you hope,
(of love, nor does she hope for it,)

akɛsa βakɛɾa
aquessa vaquera
that milkmaid

ðɛ la finɔxɔsa
de la Finojosa."
from Finojosa."

Idiomatic translation:
    I was traveling from Calatraveño to Santa Maria when I saw a beautiful milkmaid from Finojosa. Because I was tired and sleepy, I had lost my way when I found her. In a meadow of roses, guarding the cattle, I could hardly believe that she was the milkmaid from Finojosa. Spring roses could not be as lovely as that milkmaid from Finojosa. I could hardly look at her great beauty because I was unattached and I wanted her to be mine. With courage, I said, "Charming," because I knew who she was, the milkmaid from Finojosa.
    She laughingly said, "Well, come. I understand what you want. I don't desire love nor do I hope for it because I am the milkmaid from Finojosa."

arβɔl
4. Árbol (1987)
Tree

Fina de Calderón

Fina de Calderón is the pseudonym of Josefina Attar, the daughter of the industrialist Rafael Attar. Born in Madrid, she is a good friend of the Rodrigos and continues to write poetry in Toledo, Spain.[3]

Fina de Calderón is an institution in the social and cultural life of Madrid. She holds a title of nobility, Marquesa de Mozabamba, and is well known as a poet, wirter and composer of music. She is an old friend of Victoria and Joaquín Rodrigo from their years as students in Paris.[4]

arβɔl flɔɾeθɛmɛ ɔtɾɔ swɛɲɔ
Árbol, floréceme otro sueño,
Tree, bloom for me another dream,

la tarðɛz ɣɾana
la tarde es grana,
the afternoon is scarlet,

i tu sɛɾaz mi trɔŋkɔ
y tú serás mi tronco
and you will be my tree trunk

i jɔ tu rama akɔlɔɾaða
y yo tu rama acolorada.
and I your branch colored.
(and I your colored branch.)

arβɔl flɔɾeθɛmɛ ɔtɾɔ swɛɲɔ
Árbol, floréceme otro sueño,
Tree, bloom for me another dream,

duɾantɛl alβa
durante el alba,
during the dawn,

i jɔ sɛɾɛ tu aβɾaθɔ
y yo seré tu abrazo,
and I will be your embrace,

kɔrtɛθa βlaŋka ðuɾantɛl alβa
corteza blanca durante el alba,
bark white during the dawn,
(white bark during the dawn,)

blaŋka ðɛ fɾutɔ
blanca de fruto,
white of fruit,

rɔxa ðɛ ʎama
roja de llama.
red of flame.

Idiomatic translation:
    Tree, make another dream for me as the afternoon becomes
evening. You will be my trunk and I will be your branch. During
dawn, I will be your embrace, white bark, white fruit, and red flame.

pɔr kɛ tɛ ʎamaɾɛ
5. ¿Por qué te llamaré? (1987)
Why Would I Call You?

Fina de Calderón

pɔr kɛ tɛ ʎamaɾɛ jɔ
¿Por qué te llamaré yo
For what you I will call
(Why would I call you)

mi ɣɾanitɔ ðɛ kafɛ kafɛ
mi granito de café, café,
my small grain of coffee, coffee,
(my little grain of coffee,)

si tjɛnɛs ɛl pɛlɔ ruβjɔ
si tienes el pelo rubio
if you have the hair blond
(when your hair is blond)

i tjɛnɛz βlaŋka la pjɛl la pjɛl
y tienes blanca la piel, la piel?
and you have white the skin, the skin?
(and your skin is white?)

pɔr kɛ tɛ ʎamaɾɛ jɔ
¿Por qué te llamaré yo
For what you I will call
(Why would I call you)

mi pɛδaθitɔ δɛ pan δɛ pan
mi pedacito de pan, de pan,
my little slice of bread, of bread,

sjɛl ambɾɛ δɛ tu kaɾiɲɔ
si el hambre de tu cariño
if the hunger of your affection

nɔ mɛ la pwɛδɛs kitar
no me la puedes quitar?
not to me it you can remove?
(you will not let me leave it behind?)

pɔr kɛ tɛ ʎamaɾɛ jɔ
¿Por qué te llamaré yo
For what you I will call
(Why would I call you)

mi luθɛɾɔ mi klaβɛl klaβɛl
mi lucero o mi clavel, clavel,
my bright star or my carnation, carnation,

si kwandɔ ɛstas fɾɛntɛ a ɛʎɔs
si cuando estás frente a ellos
if when you are in front of them

ni astɾɔs ni flɔɾɛs sɛ βɛn sɛ βɛn
ni astros ni flores se ven, se ven?
neither stars nor flowers are seen, are seen?

Idiomatic translation:
    Why will I call you my little grain of coffee when you have blond

hair and white skin?

Why will I call you my little slice of bread if you will not let me leave behind the hunger of your affection.

Why will I call you my shining star or my carnation if when you are in front of them, neither can be seen?

Notes

1. Philip Ward, ed., The Oxford *Companion to Spanish Literature* (Oxford: Clarendon Press, 1978), 606.

2. Ward, Oxford *Companion*, 531.

3. Fina de Calderon, *Fuego, grito, luna: Federico Garcia Lorca: poema en tres letras/de Fina de Calderon* (Malaga: Ediciones Litoral, 1977), 5-6.

4. Cecilia Rodrigo, E-mail to the author, October 5, 1998.

Chapter 5

Cantos de amor y de guerra

kantɔz ðɛ amɔr i ðɛ ɣɛrra
Cantos de amor y de guerra (1969)

Songs of Love and War	12:05
Paseábase el rey moro	3:30
¡A las armas, moriscotes!	2:00
·¡Ay, luna que reluces!	2:00
Sobre Baza estaba el rey	3:10
Pastorcico, tú que has vuelto	1:25

Vocal Range: D^4 to G^5
For voice and piano or voice and orchestra
Orchestra: harp, flutes, oboes, horn, and trumpet

This cycle of five songs was composed for and dedicated to Cecilia Rodrigo, the only daughter of Joaquín Rodrigo and his wife, Victoria Kamhi. It was commissioned by the National Radio and was premiered in March 1969, by Ana Higueras, soprano and Odón Alonso, conductor.[1] The set was originally composed for orchestra, but with Rodrigo's approval, a piano reduction was arranged by Vicente Asencio, the Valencian composer and disciple of Morera and Turina. This reduction was later revised by Victoria Kamhi. The

111

songs are inspired by ballads and medieval romances dealing with
love or the border fighting with the Moors. The music and texts were
adapted by Victoria Kamhi from the sixteenth-century Cancioneros.

Cecilia Rodrigo writes:

Cantos de amor y de guerra was dedicated to me as a gift, as
were other works as well. With his characteristic sense of
humor, as I had been married for five years at the time, Rodrigo
made a parallelism of love and war in the state of matrimony!
Some of the romances included in this collection I used to recite
at school.[2]

paseaβase εl rεj mɔɾɔ
1. **Paseábase el rey moro**
The King of the Moors passed by

paseaβase εl rεj mɔɾɔ
Paseábase el rey moro
Passes the King Moorish
(The Moorish King traveled)

pɔr la θjuðað ðε ɣɾanaða
por la ciudad de Granada,
through the city of Granada

kartaz lε fwεɾɔm beniðas
cartas le fueron venidas
letters him telling had come
(letters telling him had come)

kɔmɔ alama εɾa ɣanaða
cómo Alhama era ganada.
how Alhama was won.

a mi alama
¡Ah, mi Alhama!
Ah! my Alhama!

Idiomatic translation:
    The Moorish King was traveling through the city of Granada. He
had received letters telling him how Alhama was won. Ay!

"Paseábase el rey moro" is a ballad imitating Arabic poetry. It was written perhaps as early as the fourteenth century and may refer to an incident in June 886, when Omar, son of Hafsun, defeated the Moors in battle at Alhama. Omar extended his domain, and in effect, became King of Southern Spain.[3]

However, Binkley and Frenk[4] believe this story dates to February 28, 1482, when the Marqués of Cádiz, Don Rodrigo Ponce de León, was able to take the Moorish city of Alhama. According to the ballad, his able soldier Juan de Ortega silently scaled the city wall and enabled the defeat of the Moorish king. These researchers explain the reconstruction of the text, present the Bernal Gonçález/Fuenllana song arrangement, and supply a more complete text.

This poem, like the fourth one in the cycle ("Sobre Baza"), is one of a large number of ballads composed on Moorish themes. After the final overthrow of Moorish power in 1492, poets were inspired by tales of war and disasters at cities like Baza, Ronda, and Alhama. The subjects involve known occurrences but are rarely historical. Instead, these ballads are wildly imaginative and link the present with an ancient, but glorious, event.

"Paseábase el rey moro" is remarkably different from the others in this set because of its use of ragas, or repeated melodic fragments, rhythmic "talas," and vocal grace notes, all inherent to Hindu music. The influence of Arabian and Moorish music is apparent in the long introduction and postlude, simple in nature, but designed to create suspense and tension. Hindu and Arabic characteristics are also seen in the transparent accompaniment of the vocal line. All attention is drawn to the melismatic melody, so that the meaning of the text is intensified. The vocal ornaments, with their ancient Moorish history, create a disconsolate lament appropriate for the text.

a las armaz moɻiskɔtɛs

II. ¡A las armas, moriscotes!
To arms, Moriscotes!

a las armaz moɻiskɔtɛs

A las armas, moriscotes,
To the arms, Moors,
(To arms, Moriscotes,)

si lɔ an ɛm bɔluntaȍ

si lo han en voluntad,
if it you have of desire,
(if you wish to fight,)

kɛ si tɛntran lɔs franθɛsɛs
que si te entran los franceses,
so that if enter the French

lɔs kɛn rɔmɛɾia βan
los que en romería van.
those who on pilgrimage go.
(those who are on pilgrimage.)

Idiomatic translation:
    Take up arms, moriscotes, if you do it willingly, in case the
French come here on pilgrimage. (Moriscotes were Spanish Moors
who accepted Christianity.)
    There is a textual misprint in the Union Musical Ediciones,
printed in 1991. It occurs in the second line of the poem, which
should read "si lo han en voluntad," rather than "si lo has de
voluntad."

aj luna kɛ rɛluθɛs
III. ¡Ay, luna que reluces!
Oh, moon that gleams!

aj luna kɛ rɛluθɛs
¡Ay, luna que reluces,
Oh, moon that gleams,

tɔða la nɔtʃɛ mɛ alumbɾɛs
toda la noche me alumbres!
all the night me illuminates!

aj luna tam bɛʎa
¡Ay, luna tan bella,
Oh moon so pretty,

alumbɾɛz mɛ a la ɣɛrra
alúmbres me a la guerra,
illuminate me to the war,

pɔr ðɔ βaja i βɛŋga
por do vaya y venga
for where goes and comes

tɔða la nɔtʃɛ mɛ alumbɾɛs
toda la noche me alumbres...
all the night me illuminates...

Idiomatic translation:
Oh, moon that gleams, all night you illuminate me. Oh, moon so pretty, you brighten all for me at war. Wherever I go and come, all night you illuminate me...

sɔβɾɛ βaθa ɛstaβa ɛl ɾɛj
IV. **Sobre Baza estaba el rey**
The King was on Baza

sɔβɾɛ βaθa ɛstaβa ɛl ɾɛj
Sobre Baza estaba el Rey,
On Baza was the King
(The King was on Baza)

lunɛz ðɛspwɛz ðɛ jantar
lunes, después de yantar;
Monday, after eating;

miɾaβa laz rikas tjɛndas
miraba las ricas tiendas
he looked at the rich tents

kɛstaβan ɛn su ɾɛal
que estaban en su real;
that were in his realm;

miɾaβa las wɛrtaz ɣɾandɛs
miraba las huertas grandes
he looked at the vegetable gardens large
(he looked at the large vegetable gardens)

i miɾaβa ɛl arraβal
y miraba el arrabal,
and he looked at the outer surroundings,

miɾaβa ɛl aðarβɛ fwɛrtɛ
miraba el adarve fuerte
he looked at the parapet strong
(he looked at the strong parapet)

kɛ tɛnia la θjuðað
que tenía la ciudad;
that held the city;

miɾaβa las tɔrrɛs ɛspɛsas
miraba las torres espesas
he looked at the towers thick
(he looked at the thick towers)

kɛ nɔ las pwɛðɛ kɔntar
que no las puede contar.
that not them he could count.
(that were too numerous to count.)

um mɔɾɔ tras unalmɛna
Un moro, tras una almena,
A moor behind a parapet,

kɔmɛnθɔlɛ ðɛ faβlar
comenzóle de fablar;
began to speak;

bɛtɛ ɛl rɛj fɛrnandɔ
"Vete, el Rey Fernando,
" Go away, (the) King Fernando,

nɔn kjɛɾas akimbɛrnar
non quieras aquí invernar,
not you wish here to stay,
(you do not wish to stay here,)

kɛ lɔs fɾiɔz ðɛsta tjɛrra
que los fríos de esta tierra
that the cold of this earth
(the cold of this earth)

nɔ lɔs pɔðɾas kɔmpɔrtar
no los podrás comportar."
not it will be able to tolerate."
(you will not be able to tolerate.")

pan tɛnɛmɔs pɔr ðjɛθ aɲɔs
Pan tenemos por diez años;
Bread we have for ten years;
(we have enough bread for ten years;)

mil βakas paɾa salar
mil vacas para salar;
a thousand cows to salt;

bɛjntɛ mil mɔɾɔs aj ðɛntrɔ
veinte mil moros hay dentro,
twenty thousand moors there are inside

tɔðɔz ðɛ armas tɔmar
todos de armas tomar,
all of arms to take up,
(ready to take up arms,)

ɔtʃɔθjɛntɔz ðɛ a kaβaʎɔ
ochocientos de a caballo
eight hundred of horses
(eight hundred horses)

paɾa ɛl ɛskaɾamuθar
para el escaramuzar
for the battle
(ready for battle)

sjɛtɛ kauðiʎɔs tɛnɛmɔs
siete caudillos tenemos,
seven leaders we have,

tam bwɛnɔs kɔmɔ rɔldan
tan buenos como Roldan,
as good as Roland (the great French leader),

i xuɾamɛntɔ tjɛnɛn fɛtʃɔ
y juramento tienen fecho
and oaths they have made

antɛz mɔɾir kɛ sɛ ðar
¡"antes morir que se dar!"
" before death that they won't surrender!"

Idiomatic translation:
    The King was on Baza, and Monday after eating, he looked at the rich tents in his realm; he looked at the big gardens, the outer surroundings, and the city's parapet walk. He looked at the numerous, thick towers. A Moor behind a parapet began to speak to him: "Go away, King Fernando. You don't want to spend the winter here because you won't be able to stand the cold of this land. We have food for ten years; a thousand cows to salt down; there are twenty thousand Moors inside, all ready to take up arms. We have eight hundred on horseback and for battle, we have seven leaders as good as Roland, and they have sworn that they will fight until death!"

    King Fernando, the principal character in "Sobre Baza," ruled about the middle of the eleventh century. He was successful in many battles against the Moors and regained many cities from them.[5]
    Again, there is a misprint in the text in the Union Musicales Ediciones, printed 1991. The line "non quieras aquí invermar," should read, "non quieras aquí invernar."

pastɔrθikɔ tu kɛ az βwɛltɔ
V. **Pastorcico, tú que has vuelto**
Little shepherd, you who have returned

pastɔrθikɔ tu kɛ az βwɛltɔ
Pastorcico, tú que has vuelto
Little shepherd, you who have returned

dɛ lɔ altɔ ðɛsa mɔntaɲa
de lo alto de esa montaña
from the height of that mountain

dime tu βwɛn pastɔrθikɔ
dime tú, buen pastorcico,
tell me you, good little shepherd
(tell me, good little shepherd)

si aʎastɛ a mjɛnamɔɾaδa
si hallaste a mi enamorada.
if you found my beloved.

Idiomatic translation:
Little shepherd, you have returned from the highest point of the mountain. Tell me, good shepherd, if you have found my loved one.

Notes

1. Victoria Kamhi, *Hand in Hand with Joaquín Rodrigo, My Life at the Maestro's Side,* trans. Ellen Wilkerson (Pittsburgh: Latin American Literary Review Press, 1992), 228.
2. Cecilia Rodrigo, E-mail to author, April 23, 1998.
3. Reinhart Dozy, *Spanish Islam: A History of the Moslems in Spain,* trans. Frances Griffin Stokes (New York: Duffield, 1913), 316-321.
4. Thomas Binkley and Margit Frenk, *Spanish Romances of the Sixteenth Century* (Bloomington: Indiana University Press, 1995), 107-109.
5. Dozy, *Spanish Islam,* 654.

Chapter 6

Con Antonio Machado

Con Antonio Machado (1970)	24:45
With Antonio Machado	
Preludio	3:25
Mi corazón te aguarda	2:50
Tu voz y tu mano	2:00
Mañana de abril	4:00
Los sueños	2:00
Cantaban los niños	3:00
¿Recuerdas?	2:45
Fiesta en el prado	1:45
Abril galán	1:00
Canción del Duero	2:00

Vocal Range: C^4 to G^5
For voice and piano

In 1972, Rodrigo and Federico Mompou were both commissioned by the Ministry of Education to compose a song cycle for soprano and piano. Maestro Rodrigo selected poems by Antonio Machado and quickly composed this song cycle. It was premiered in October 1972, in Seville by María Orán.[1]

Antonio Machado (1875-1939) is considered one of the most outstanding poets of Spain since the seventeenth century. He taught

French in the secondary school system and was sent to teach in Soria, a town in the mountains of Old Castile. In 1909, Machado married Leonor Izquierdo, the fifteen-year-old daughter of a retired policeman. Her death three years later nearly drove Machado to suicide. Machado's early poems exhibit a post--Symbolist spirit. His poems, generally, are attentive to landscape and nature, folklore, and are imbued with images of water--fountains, rivers, and so on--all of which symbolize the stream of time. Leonor's death, in his poetry, is expressed as "love as an emotion compatible with solitude and nourished mainly on absence." 2

pæluðjɔ
Preludio
Prelude

mjɛntɾaz la sɔmbɾa pasa ðɛ un santɔ amɔr ɔj kjɛɾɔ
Mientras la sombra pasa de un santo amor, hoy quiero
While the shade passes from a sacred love, today I wish

pɔnɛɾ un dulθɛ salmɔ sɔβɾɛ mi βjɛxɔ atɾil
poner un dulce salmo sobre mi viejo atril.
to put a sweet Psalm on my old music stand.

akɔɾðaɾɛ laz nɔtaz ðɛl ɔɾɣanɔ sɛβɛɾɔ
Acordaré las notas del órgano severo
I will harmonize the notes of the organ strict
(I will harmonize the notes of the strict organ)

al suspiɾar fɾaɣantɛ ðɛl pifanɔ ðɛ aβɾil
al suspirar fragante del pífano de abril.
to the sigh fragrant of the fife of April.
(to the fragrant sigh of April's fife.)

maðuɾaɾan su aɾoma las pɔmas ɔtɔɲalɛs
Madurarán su aroma las pomas otoñales,
They will ripen its aroma the apples autumn,
(The autumn apples will ripen their aroma,)

la mirra jɛl inθjɛnsɔ salmɔðjaɾan su ɔlɔr
la mirra y el incienso salmodiarán su olor;
the myrrh and the incense will chant their smell;

ɛksalaɾan su fɾɛskɔ pɛrfumɛ lɔz rɔsalɛs
exhalarán su fresco perfume los rosales
will exhale its fresh perfume the rose bushes.
(the rose bushes will exhale their fresh perfume.)

baxɔ las paθ ɛn sɔmbɾa ðɛl tiβjɔ wɛrtɔ ɛɱ flɔr
bajo las paz en sombra del tibio huerto en flor.
below the peace in the shade of the warm orchard in bloom.

al ɣɾaβɛ akɔrðɛ lɛntɔ ðɛ musika jaɾɔma
Al grave acorde lento de música y aroma
To the serious chord slow of music and smell

la sɔlaj βjɛxaj nɔβlɛ raθɔn dɛ mi rɛθar
la sola y vieja y noble razón de mi rezar
the only and old and noble reason of my prayer

lɛβantaɾa su βwɛlɔ swaβɛ ðɛ palɔma
levantará su vuelo suave de paloma,
shall raise its flight smooth of the dove,

i la palaβɾa βlaŋka sɛlɛβaɾal altar
y la palabra blanca se elevará al altar.
and the word white it will be raised to the altar.
(and the white word will be raised to the altar.)

Idiomatic translation:
   While the shade passes from a sacred love, today I want to put a sweet Psalm on my old music stand. I will harmonize the notes at the organ while April's fife breathes fragrant sighs. The autumn apples will ripen and the myrrh and incense will chant their smell; the rosebushes will exhale their fresh perfume to create peace in the shade of the warm orchard in bloom. To the serious chord, slow of music and smell, the single, old, and noble reason of my prayer shall be to ascend like the smooth flight of the dove and the white word will be raised to the altar.

mi kɔɾaθɔn tɛ aɣwarða
Mi corazón te aguarda
My heart you awaits
(My Heart Awaits You)

amaða ɛl auɾa ðiθɛ
Amada, el aura dice
Beloved, the breeze says

tu puɾa βɛstɛ βlaŋka
tu pura veste blanca...
your pure dress white...
(your pure white dress...)

nɔ tɛ βɛɾam mis ɔxɔs
No te verán mis ojos:
No you they will see my eyes:
(my eyes will not see you:)

mi kɔɾaθɔn tɛ aɣwarða
¡Mi corazón te aguarda!
My heart you awaits!
(My heart awaits you!)

ɛl βjɛntɔ mɛ a tɾaiðɔ
El viento me ha traído
The wind to me has brought
(The wind has brought to me)

tu nɔmbɾɛn la maɲana
tu nombre en la mañana;
your name in the morning;

ɛl ɛkɔ ðɛ tus pasɔz
el eco de tus pasos
the echo of your steps

rɛpitɛ la mɔntaɲa
repite la montaña...
repeats the mountains...
(the mountains repeat...)

nɔ tɛ βɛɾam mis ɔxɔs
No te verán mis ojos;
No you they will see my eyes;
(My eyes will not see you;)

mi kɔɾaθɔn tɛ aɣwarða
¡**mi corazón te aguarda!**
My heart you awaits!
(My heart awaits you!)

ɛn las sɔmbɾias tɔrrɛz
En las sombrías torres
In the gloomy towers

rɛpikan las kampanas
repican las campanas...
peal the bells...
(the bells peal...)

nɔ tɛ βɛɾam mis ɔxɔs
No te verán mis ojos;
No you they will not see my eyes;
(My eyes will not see you;)

mi kɔɾaθɔn tɛ aɣwarða
¡**mi corazón te aguarda!**
My heart you awaits!
(My heart awaits you!)

lɔz ɣɔlpɛz ðɛl martiʎɔ
Los golpes del martillo
The blows of the hammer

ðiθɛn la nɛɣɾa kaxa
dicen la negra caja;
say the black chest,

jɛl sitjɔ ðɛ la fɔsa
y el sitio de la fosa,
and the place of the pit (grave),

lɔz ɣɔlpɛz ðɛ la aθaða
los golpes de la azada...
the blows of the hoe...

nɔ tɛ βɛɾam mis ɔxɔs
No te verán mis ojos;
No you they will not see my eyes;
(My eyes will not see you;)

mi kɔɾaθɔn tɛ aɣwarða
¡Mi corazón te aguarda!
My heart you awaits!
(My heart awaits you!)

Idiomatic translation:
My heart waits for you but my eyes will not see you. The breeze calls you beloved, and I remember your lovely white dress. The wind whispers your name and the mountains resound with your footsteps, but my eyes will not see you. The bells ring in the somber towers as my body is lowered into the grave. My heart waits for you but my eyes are not able to see you.

tu βɔθ i tu manɔ
Tu voz y tu mano
Your Voice and Your Hand

sɔɲɛ kɛ tu mɛ ʎɛβaβas
Soñé que tú me llevabas
I dreamed that you me carried
(I dreamed that you carried me)

pɔr una βlaŋka βɛɾɛða
por una blanca vereda,
across a white path,

ɛm mɛðjɔ ðɛl kampɔ βɛrðɛ
en medio del campo verde,
in the middle of the countryside green,
(in the middle of the green countryside,)

aθja ɛl aθul dɛ las sjɛrras
hacia el azul de las sierras,
towards the blue of the mountains,

aθja lɔz mɔntɛs aθulɛs
hacia los montes azules,
toward the mountains blue,
(toward the blue mountains,)

una maɲana sɛɾɛna
una mañana serena.
a morning serene.
(a serene morning.)

sɛnti tu mano ɛn la mia
Sentí tu mano en la mía,
I felt your hand in mine,

tu manɔ ðɛ kɔmpaɲɛɾa
tu mano de compañera,
your hand of companionship,

tu βɔz ðɛ niɲa ɛm mi ɔiðɔ
tu voz de niña en mi oído
your voice of the girl in my hearing
(your girl's voice in my hearing)

kɔmɔ una kampana nwɛβa
como una campana nueva,
like a bell new,
(like a new bell,)

kɔmɔ una kampana βirxɛn
como una campana virgen
like a bell virgin
(like a virgin bell)

dɛ un alβa ðɛ pɾimaβɛɾa
de un alba de primavera.
of a dawn of spring.
(of a spring dawn.)

ɛɾan tu βɔθ i tu manɔ
¡Eran tu voz y tu mano,
They were your voice and your hand,

ɛn swɛɲɔs tam bɛrðaðɛɾas
en sueños, tan verdaderas!...
in dreams, so genuine!...

biβɛspɛɾanθa kjɛn saβɛ
Vive, esperanza: ¡quién sabe
Live, hope: who knows

lɔ kɛ sɛ tɾaɣa la tjɛrra
lo que se traga la tierra!
it that itself swallows the earth!
(that which swallows the earth!)

Idiomatic translation:
   One serene morning, I dreamed that you carried me across a white path through the green countryside toward the blue mountains. I felt your hand in mine and heard your voice in my ears. Your voice was like a new bell, a virgin bell, the dawn of spring. In my dream, your voice and the touch of your hand were so real! Who can know what the earth will take away!

maɲana ðɛ aβɾil
Mañana de abril
Morning of April
(April Morning)

ɛɾa una maɲana jaβɾil sɔnɾeia
Era una mañana y abril sonreía
It was a morning and April smiled

fɾɛntɛ al ɔɾiθɔntɛ ðɔɾaðɔ mɔɾia
Frente al horizonte dorado moría
In front of the horizontal purple was dying

la luna muj βlaŋka jɔpaka tɾas ɛʎa
la luna, muy blanca y opaca; tras ella,
the moon, very white and opaque; behind her,

kwal tɛnwɛ lixɛɾa kimɛɾa kɔrria
cual tenue ligera quimera, corría
like tenuous light hallucination, it flowed

la nuβɛ kɛ apɛnas ɛnturβja una ɛstɾɛʎa
la nube que apenas enturbia una estrella.
the cloud that hardly made cloudy a star.

kɔmɔ sɔnrɛia la rɔsa maɲana
Como sonreía la rosa mañana
How smiled the pink morning
(How the pink morning smiled)

al sɔl dɛl ɔɾjɛntɛ aβɾi mi βɛntana
al sol del Oriente abrí mi ventana;
to the sun of the East I opened my window;

jɛm mi tɾistɛ alkɔβa pɛnɛtɾɔ ɛl ɔɾjɛntɛ
y en mi triste alcoba penetró el Oriente
and into my sad bedroom penetrated the East

ɛŋ kantɔ ðɛ alɔndɾas ɛn risa ðɛ fwɛntɛ
en canto de alondras, en risa de fuente
in a song of larks, in the laughter of fountains

jɛn swaβɛ pɛrfumɛ ðɛ flɔɾa tɛmpɾana
y en suave perfume de flora temprana.
and in soft perfume of flower early.
(and in the soft perfume of the early flower.)

fwɛ una klaɾa tarðɛ ðɛ mɛlaŋkɔlia
Fue una clara tarde de melancolía.
It was a clear afternoon of melancholy.

aβɾil sɔnrɛia jɔ aβɾi laz βɛntanaz
Abril sonreía. Yo abrí las ventanas
April smiled. I opened the windows

ðɛ mi kasal βjɛntɔ ɛl βjɛntɔ tɾaia
de mi casa al viento...El viento traía
of my house to the wind...The wind carried

pɛrfumɛ ðɛ rɔsas dɔβlar ðɛ kampanas
perfume de rosas, doblar de campanas...
perfume of roses, tolling of bells...

dɔβlar ðε kampanas lεxanas ʎɔɾɔsas
Doblar de campanas lejanas, llorosas,
Tolling of bells far-away, crying,

swaβε ðε rɔsas aɾɔmaðɔ aljεntɔ
suave de rosas aromado aliento...
mild of roses aroma breath...
(mild with the aromatic breath of roses...)

dɔndεstan lɔs wεrtɔs flɔɾiðɔz ðε rɔsas
...¿Dónde están los huertos floridos de rosas?
...Where are the orchards flowering of roses?

kε ðiθεn laz ðulθεs kampanas al βjεntɔ
¿Qué dicen las dulces campanas al viento?
What say the sweet bells to the wind?

pɾεɣuntε a la tarðε ðε aβɾil kε mɔɾia
Pregunté a la tarde de abril que moría:
I asked the afternoon of April that was dying:

al fin lalεɣɾia sε aθεrka mi kasa
¿Al fin la alegría se acerca a mi casa?
At the end happiness will it come near to my house?

la tarðε ðε aβɾil sɔnriɔ lalεɣɾia
La tarde de abril sonrió: La alegría
The afternoon of April smiled: The happiness

pasɔ pɔr tu pwεrta i lwεɣa sɔmbɾia
pasó por tu puerta—y luego, sombría;
passed by your door--and then, it became gloomy;

pasɔ pɔr tu pwεrta dɔz βεθεz nɔ pasa
pasó por tu puerta. Dos veces no pasa.
it passed by your door. Two times not passes
(Two times it does not pass.)

Idiomatic translation:
    On an April morning, the moon set in front of a purple sky. A
transparent cloud created a wispy hallucination of light. To the pink
glow of the morning, I opened my bedroom window. I heard the

Con Antonio Machado   131

lark's song, the laughter of the fountains, and I smelled the sweet perfume of the spring flowers. The melancholy afternoon brought the scent of roses and the ringing of bells through my windows. The mournful bells, the aroma of roses...What do the bells say to the wind? Where are the roses? I asked the April afternoon if happiness will come to my house. It smiled and said, "Happiness passed by your door. But it does not come twice."

lɔs swɛɲɔs
Los sueños
The Dreams

ɛl aða mas ɛrmɔsa sɔnrɛiðɔ
El hada más hermosa ha sonreido
The fairy most beautiful she has smiled
(The most beautiful fairy smiled)

al βɛr la lumbɾɛ ðɛ una ɛstɾɛʎa paliða
al ver la lumbre de una estrella pálida,
to see the light of a star pale,
(upon seeing the light of a pale star,)

kɛn ilɔ swaβɛ βlaŋkɔ i silɛnθjɔsɔ
que en hilo suave, blanco y silencioso
that in thread gentle, white and silent

sɛnrɔskal usɔ ðɛ su ruβja ɛrmana
se enrosca al huso de su rubia hermana.
itself twists to the spindle of her blond sister.
(twists itself to the spindle of her blond sister.)

i βwɛlβɛ a sɔnrɛir pɔrkɛn su rwɛka
Y vuelve a sonreir, porque en su rueca
And she returns to smiling, because in her spinning wheel

ɛl ilɔ ðɛ lɔs kampɔs sɛmmaɾaɲa
el hilo de los campos se enmaraña.
the thread of the countryside itself is entangled.

tɾaz la tɛnwɛ kɔrtina ðɛ lalkɔβa
Tras la tenue cortina de la alcoba,
Behind the thin curtain of the bedroom,

ɛsta ɛl xarðin ɛmbwɛltɔ ɛn luz ðɔɾaða
está el jardín envuelto en luz dorada.
lies the garden wrapped up in light golden.

la kuna kasi ɛn sɔmbra ɛl niɲɔ ðwɛrmɛ
La cuna, casi en sombra. El niño duerme.
The cradle, almost in shade. The boy is sleeping.

dɔs aðaz laβɔɾjɔsaz lɔ akɔmpaɲan
Dos hadas laboriosas lo acompañan,
Two fairies industriously him accompany,

ilandɔ ðɛ lɔs swɛɲɔz lɔs sutilɛs
hilando de los sueños los sutiles
spinning from his dreams the subtle

kɔpɔs ɛn rwɛkaz ðɛ marfil i plata
copos en ruecas de marfil y plata.
lumps on the spinning wheel of ivory and silver.

Idiomatic translation:
    A beautiful fairy smiled to see the light from a pale star twist itself
to her sister's spindle. The fairy smiles again, because the thread of
the countryside entwines itself also to her spinning wheel. As the boy
lies sleeping in the cradle, the garden is wrapped in golden light.
Two fairies spin his dreams from ivory and silver threads on the
spinning wheel.

kantaβan lɔz niɲɔs
Cantaban los niños
Were Singing the Children
(The Children Were Singing)

jɔ ɛskutʃɔ lɔs kantɔz ðɛ βjɛxas kaðɛnθjas
Yo escucho los cantos de viejas cadencias,
I listen to the songs of the old cadences,

kɛ kantan lɔz niɲɔs kwandɔ ɛŋ kɔrrɔ xwɛɣan
que cantan los niños cuando en corro juegan,
that sing the children while in a circle they play,
(that the children sing while they play in a circle,)

i βjɛrtɛn ɛŋ kɔrɔ sus almas kɛ swɛɲan
y vierten en coro sus almas que sueñan
and spill in chorus their souls that dream

kwal βjɛrtɛn sus aɣwaz las fwɛntɛz ðɛ pjɛðɾa
cual vierten sus aguas las fuentes de piedra.
which spill over their waters the fountains of stone.
(which their waters spill over the stone fountains.)

kɔm mɔnɔtɔniaz ðɛ risas ɛtɛrnas
Con monotonías de risas eternas
With the monotony of laughter eternal
(With the monotony of eternal laughter)

kɛ nɔ sɔn alɛɣɾɛs kɔn layɾimaz βjɛxas
que no son alegres, con lágrimas viejas,
that not are happy, with tears old,
(that are not happy, with old tears,)

kɛ nɔ sɔn amarɣas i ðiθɛn tɾistɛθas
que no son amargas y dicen tristezas,
that not they are bitter and they say sadness,
(that are not bitter and they say sadness,)

tɾistɛθaz ðɛ amɔɾɛz ðɛ antiɣwaz lɛjɛndas
tristezas de amores de antiguas leyendas.
sadness of loves from ancient legends.

ɛn lɔz laβjɔz niɲɔs las kanθjɔnɛz ʎɛβan
En los labios niños, las canciones llevan
On the lips children, the songs they carry
(On the children's lips, the songs they carry)

kɔɲfusa la istɔɾja i klaɾa la pɛna
confusa la historia y clara la pena:
confused the story and clear the pain
(the confused story and the clear pain)

kɔmɔ klaɾa ɛl aɣwa ʎɛβa su kɔnsɛxa
como clara el agua lleva su conseja
like clear the water it takes away its advice
(like the clear water it takes away its advice)

ðɛ βjɛxɔs amɔɾɛs kɛ nuŋka sɛ kwɛntan
de viejos amores, que nunca se cuentan.
of old loves, that never are told.
(of old loves, that are never told.)

xuɣandɔ a la sɔmbɾa ðɛ un plaθa βjɛxa
Jugando a la sombra de un plaza vieja,
Playing in the shade of a plaza old,
(Playing in the shade of an old plaza,)

lɔz niɲɔs kantaβan la fwɛntɛ ðɛ pjɛðra
los niños cantaban...La fuente de piedra
the children were singing...The fountain of stone

bɛrtia su ɛtɛrnɔ kristal dɛ lɛjɛnda
vertía su eterno cristal de leyenda.
spills its eternal crystal of legend.
(spills its eternal crystal legend.)

kantaβan lɔz niɲɔs kanθjɔnɛs iŋxɛnwas
Cantaban los niños canciones ingenuas,
Were singing the children songs simple,
(The children were singing simple songs,)

dɛ un alɣɔ kɛ pasa i kɛ nuŋka ʎɛɣa
de un algo que pasa y que nunca llega:
of a something that passes and that never arrives:

la istɔɾja kɔɲfusa i kaɾa la pɛna
la historia confusa y clara la pena.
the story confused and clear the pain.
(the confused story and the clear pain.)

sɛɣia su kwɛntɔ la fwɛntɛ sɛɾena
Seguía su cuento la fuente serena;
It continued its tale the fountain serene;
(The serene fountain continued its tale;)

bɔrraða la istɔɾja kɔntaβa la pɛna
borrada la historia, contaba la pena.
erased the story, told the pain.

Idiomatic translation:
I listen to the songs the children sing. While they sing and dance, their songs tell of their fondest dreams, like the waters that flow over stone fountains, echo the monotony of ancient laughter. The fountain, like the children and their songs, is sad with old tears. They both tell the tales of sad loves from ancient legends.

The children's songs confuse the stories but the pain is clear. The fountain's waters wash away the stories of old, secret loves. In the shade of the old plaza, the children sing and play while the crystal fountain spills its eternal legend.

The simple songs tell of something that passes and yet never arrives. The confused story tells of the pain. The serene fountain continued the story and sobbed the pain.

rɛkwɛrðas
¿Recuerdas?
Do you Remember?

mi amɔr rɛkwɛrðas dimɛ
¿Mi amor?... ¿Recuerdas, dime,
My love?...Do you remember, tell me,

akɛʎɔs xuŋkɔs tjɛrnɔs
aquellos juncos tiernos,
those reeds tender,
(those tender reeds,)

laŋyiðɔs i amaɾiʎɔs
lánguidos y amarillos
languid and yellow

kɛ aj ɛn ɛl kauθɛ sɛkɔ
que hay en el cauce seco?...
that are in the riverbed dry?...
(that are in the dry riverbed?...)

rɛkwɛrðaz la amapɔla
¿Recuerdas la amapola
Do you remember the poppy

kɛ kalθinɔ ɛl βɛɾanɔ
que calcinó el verano,
that blackened the summer,

la amapɔla martʃita
la amapola marchita,
the poppy whithered,
(the whithered poppy,)

nɛɣɾɔ kɾɛspɔn dɛl kampɔ
negro crespón del campo?...
black crepe of the field?...

tɛ akwɛrðaz ðɛl sɔl dʒɛrtɔ
¿Te acuerdas del sol yerto
Do you remember the sun rigid
(Do you remember the rigid sun)

i umildɛn la maɲana
y humilde, en la mañana,
and humble, in the morning,

kɛ βɾiʎa i tjɛmbla rɔtɔ
que brilla y tiembla roto
that shines and trembles broken

sɔβɾɛ una fwɛntɛlaða
sobre una fuente helada?...
on a fountain frozen?...
(on a frozen fountain?...)

Idiomatic translation:
    Do you remember, love, the tender, yellow reeds in the dry riverbed? Do you remember the withered poppy that blackened the summer fields? Do you remember the morning sun, rigid and humble, that shines and trembles on a frozen fountain?

fjɛsta ɛn ɛl pɾaðɔ
Fiesta en el prado
Fiesta in the Field

aj fjɛsta ɛn ɛl pɾaðɔ βɛɾðɛ
Hay fiesta en el prado verde
There is a fiesta in the field green
(There is a fiesta in the green field)

pifanɔ i tambɔr
–pífano y tambor––.
–fife and drum––.

kɔn su kajaðɔ flɔɾiðɔ
Con su cayado florido
With his crook ornate
(With his ornate crook)

jaβarkaz ðɛ ɔɾɔ βinɔ um pastɔr
y abarcas de oro vino un pastor.
and sandals of gold came a shepherd.
(and gold sandals, a shepherd came.)

dɛl mɔntɛ βaxɛ
Del monte bajé,
From the mountain I came,

sɔlɔ pɔr βajlar kɔn ɛʎa
sólo por bailar con ella;
alone to dance with her;

al mɔntɛ mɛ tɔrnaɾɛ
al monte me tornaré.
to the mountain I will return.

ɛn lɔs arβɔlez ðɛl wɛrtɔ
En los árboles del huerto
In the trees of the orchard

aj un rwisɛɲɔr
hay un ruiseñor;
there is a nightingale;

kanta ðɛ nɔtʃɛj ðɛ ðia
canta de noche y de día,
it sings by night and by day,

kanta la luna jal sɔl
canta a la luna y al sol,
it sings to the moon and to the sun,

rɔŋkɔ ðɛ kantar
ronco de cantar.
hoarse with singing.

al wɛrtɔ βɛndra la niɲa
"Al huerto vendrá la niña,
" To the orchard will come the girl,

juna rɔsa kɔrtaɾa
y una rosa cortará."
and a rose cut."
(and cut a rose.")

ɛntɾɛ laz nɛɣɾas ɛnθinas
Entre las negras encinas,
Among the black oaks,

aj una fwɛntɛ ðɛ pjɛðɾa
hay una fuente de piedra,
there is a fountain of stone,

juŋ kantaɾiʎɔ ðɛ βarɔ
y un cantarillo de barro
and a little pitcher of clay

kɛ nuŋka sɛ ʎɛna
que nunca se llena.
that never fills.

pɔr ɛl ɛnθinar
Por el encinar,
Through the oak grove,

kɔn la βlaŋka luna
con la blanca luna,
with the white moon,

ɛʎa βɔlβɛɾa
ella volverá.
she will return.

Idiomatic translation:
   A shepherd with gold sandals came to the fiesta in the field. I came down from the mountain to dance with her and I will return to the mountain. In the orchard, a nightingale sings night and day until it is hoarse: "The girl will come to the orchard and cut a rose." Among the black oaks, there is a fountain of stone and a pitcher of clay that can never be filled. When the white moon shines through the oak grove, she will return.

aβɾil ɣalan
Abril galán
April Gallant
(Gallant April)

mjɛntɾaz ðanθajs ɛŋ kɔrrɔ
Mientras danzais en corro,
While you dance in a circle,

niɲas kantan
niñas, cantan:
girls, sing:

ja ɛstan lɔs pɾaðɔz βɛrðɛs
"Ya están los prados verdes,
" Already they are the meadows green,
("Already the meadows are green,)

ja βinɔ aβɹil ɣalan
ya vino abril galán.
already came April gallant.
(gallant April has already come.)

a la ɔɹiʎa ðɛl riɔ
A la orilla del río
At the edge of the river

pɔr ɛl nɛɣɹɔ ɛnθinar
por el negro encinar,
by the black oak grove,

sus aβarkaz ðɛ plata
sus abarcas de plata
its sandals of silver
(April's sandals)

ɛmɔz βistɔ βɹiʎar
hemos visto brillar."
we have seen sparkle."

mjɛntɹaz ðanθajs ɛŋ kɔrrɔ
Mientras danzais en corro,
While you dance in a circle,

niɲas kantan
niñas, cantan:
girls, sing:

ja ɛstan lɔs pɹaðɔz βɛrðɛs
"Ya están los prados verdes,
" Already they are the meadows green,
("Already the meadows are green,)

ja βinɔ aβɹil ɣalan
ya vino abril galán."
already came April gallant."
(gallant April has already come.")

Idiomatic translation:
   While you dance in a circle, girls, sing: "The meadows are already green and gallant April has already come. At the river's edge, by the oak grove, we saw its silver sandals sparkle." The meadows are already green and gallant April has already come.

Kanθjɔn dɛl dwɛɾɔ
Canción del Duero
Song of the Duero (a river that flows through the Castilla y Leon region)

mɔlinɛɾɔ ɛz mi amantɛ
Molinero es mi amante;
A miller is my love;

tjɛnɛ um mɔlinɔ
tiene un molino
he has a mill

βaxɔ lɔs pinɔz βɛɾðɛs
bajo los pinos verdes,
beneath the pines green,
beneath the green pines,

θɛɾka ðɛl riɔ
cerca del río.
near to the river.

niɲas kantan
Niñas, cantan:
Girls, sing:

pɔr la ɔɾiʎa ðɛl dwɛɾɔ
"Por la orilla del Duero
" By the edge of the Duero

kisjɛɾa pasar
quisiera pasar."
I might want to pass."

pɔr las tjɛrraz ðɛ sɔɾja
Por las tierras de Soria
Through the lands of Soria
(Castila y Leon's smallest provincial capital, which stands on the
banks of the Río Duero. Machado wrote of the loveliness of the town
and its surrounding area.)

βa mi pastɔr
va mi pastor.
goes my shepherd.

si jɔ fwɛɾa una ɛnθina
¡Si yo fuera una encina
If I were an oak

sɔβɾɛ un alkɔr
sobre un alcor!
on a hill!

paɾa la sjɛsta
Para la siesta,
For his siesta,

si jɔ fwɛɾa una ɛnθina
si yo fuera una encina
if I were an oak

sɔmbɾa lɛ ðjɛɾa
sombra le diera.
shade him I would give.
(I would give him shade.)

ɛn las sjɛrraz ðɛ sɔɾja
En las sierras de Soria,
In the mountains of Soria,

aθul i njɛβɛ
azul y nieve,
blue and snow,

leɲaðɔr ɛz mi amantɛ
leñador es mi amante
the woodcutter is my love

dɛ pinɔz βɛrðɛs
de pinos verdes.
of pines green.
(of green pines.)

kjɛm fwɛɾa ɛl aɣila
¡Quién fuera el águila
She who may be an eagle
(To be an eagle)

paɾa βɛr a mi ðwɛɲɔ
para ver a mi dueño
to see my love

kɔrtandɔ ramas
cortando ramas!
cutting branches!

aj ɣaɾaβi
¡Ay, garabí!...
Oh, joy!...
(Garabí is a exclamation of great happiness)

bajlar swɛnɛ la flauta
Bailar, suene la flauta
Dance, sound the flute

jɛl tambɔɾil
y el tamboril.
and the tambourine.

Idiomatic translation:
    My love is a miller, and he has a mill beneath the green pine trees
and near the river. Sing, girls: "By the edge of the Duero I might
want to pass."
    Through the Soria mountains, my shepherd goes. If I were an oak
on a hill, I would give him shade for his siesta.
    In the blue, snowy mountains of Soria, a woodcutter is my love.

She, who may be an eagle, can see my love cutting pine branches!
Ah! Dance to the sound of the flute and tambourine!

Notes

1. Victoria Kamhi, *Hand in Hand with Joaquín Rodrigo, My Life at the Maestro's Side,* trans. Ellen Wilkerson (Pittsburgh: Latin American Literary Review Press, 1992), 237.
2. Antonio Machado *Selected Poems,* trans. Alan S. Trueblood (Cambridge: Harvard University Press, 1982), 12.

Chapter 7

Cuatre cançons en llengua catalana

kwatrɛ kənsɔns ɛn ʎɛŋgwə katalanà

Cuatre cançons en llengua catalana (1935)   11:00
Four Songs in Catalan
    Cançó del Teuladí   4:35
    Canticel   1:35
    L'Inquietut Primaveral de la Donzella   2:35
    Brollador Gentil   2:15

Vocal Range: C^4 to A-flat^5
For high voice and orchestra or high voice and piano

Orchestra: 1 piccolo, also 2nd flute, 1 flute, 1 oboe, 1 clarinet in B flat, 1 bassoon, 2 horns, 2 trumpets in C, timpani, triangle, cymbal, 2 harps, strings

In the Schott edition, the German translation by Victoria Kamhi is included. The piano reduction is by Claus-Dieter Ludwig.

"Cançó del Teuladí," Teodoro Llorente, poet, is dedicated to Carmen Andujar, an excellent soprano and the wife of "my beloved teacher," Eduardo Chavarri. "She sang many of my early songs in the 1930s and 1940s."[1]

Teodoro Llorente (1836-1911), born in Valencia, composed his poetry in Castilian until his early twenties, and then he began writing

in his native Valencian dialect. In 1878, Llorente founded Lo Rat
Penat, an important society for "lovers of the Valencian dialect."
Llorente was a great admirer of Heinrich Heine, Friedrich von
Schiller, Victor Hugo and Lord Byron and modeled his poetry in the
Romantic style. He published a literary history of Valencia in 1887.[2]

"Canticel," Josep Carner, poet, is dedicated to Gerardo Diego,
"one of the greatest 20th century Spanish poets, a member of the
generation of 27, and a good friend of mine. He wrote some
magnificent and very poetic commentaries on my music."[3]

Josep Carner I Puig-Oriol (1884-1970), born in Barcelona, revived
Catalan as a literary language. He wrote many books and short
stories, but he is also remembered for his translations into Catalan of
Shakespearean plays, stories by Hans Christian Andersen, and others.
Carner's literary works include *Primer llibre de sonets* (1905), *Bella
terra, bella gent* (1918), and *L'oreig entre les canyes* (1920). Many
younger Catalon poets were influenced by his writings.[4]

Josep Masso i Ventos is the poet of "L'Inquietut Primaveral de la
Donzella" and Joan Guasch is the poet of "Brollador Gentil."

kənsɔn dəl tɑ:ulaðɪ

1. Cançon del Teuladí
Song of the Sparrow

ʒɔjɔs kəsədɔr pəsə

Joyos cassador, passa;
Jovial hunter, pass;

buskə mes braβə kəsə

Busca mes brava cassa
pursue more brave prey

i dəʃəm kiet ə mi

I deixam quiet a mí,
and let peace to me,
(and give me peace,)

ʒɔ sɔ ləmɪk də kəzə

Jo soch l'amich de casa,
I am the friend of the house,

ʒɔ sɔ lu təːulaðɪ
Jo soch lo teuladí.
I am the sparrow.

ʒɔ no tiŋk lə plomə də lə kəðərneɾə
Jo no tinch la ploma de la cadernera
I not have the feathers of the goldfinch

kə ðɔr i ðɛ gɾanə tin lə priməβeɾə
que d'or i de grana tiny la primavera;
that the gold and the seed paints of the spring;

no tiŋk lə bɛːu ðɔlθa kə təl rrusiɲɔl
No tinch la veu dolça que te'l rossinyol;
I lack the voice sweet of the nightingale
(I lack the sweet voice of the nightingale)

ni ðə lurunɛtə ʒɔliβa ɪ ʎəːuʒəɾa
ni de l'oroneta joliva i lleugera
nor of the stork nice and the agile
(nor the nice and nimble stork)

ləs alɛs kə kruən lə mar dun sɔl bɔl
Les ales que creuen la mar d'un sol vol.
The wings that cross the sea with one flight.

də pardə əstəmɛnja sɛns flɔrs sɛnsə ʎistəs
De parda estamenya, sens flors, sense llistes,
Of the gray dress, without flowers, without stripes

bəstit pɔβrə duk
Vestit pobre duch;
dress poor I wear;
(I wear a poor dress;)

mɛs pɛnɛs i glɔrjəs əleɣrəs ɔ tristəs
Mes penes i glories, alegres o tristes,
My pains and glories, happy or sad,

ləs kəntə kɔm puk
Les cante com puch.
them I sing as I can.
(I sing them as I can.)

ləs aliɣɛs niːwən dəmun də lə rrɔkə
Les aligues niuen damunt de la roca
The eagles nest on the rock

dəl ɣɔrk kentrə timbəs ajzampla lə bɔkə
Del gorch qu'entre timbes aizampla la boca;
Of the whole that between clifts too wide the mouth;
(next to wide precipices;)

ən braŋkə fuʎɔsə lu biu pəsərɛl
En branca fullosa lo viu passarell;
In branch plenty him he sees passing;
(In leafy branches he sees him passing;)

lə torturə ən larβrə kə ʒə uβri lə sɔkə
La tórtora en l'arbre que ja obrí la soca,
The turtle dove in the tree that already opened the tree roots,

lə graʎa ən əls rrunəs dəmfunsət kəsteʎ
la gralla en els runes d'enfonsat castell.
the jackdaw in the rubble of feudal castle.

ʒɔ əl ɔmə kumfiə lə meːwə niːwaðə
Jo al home confie la meua niuada,
I to the man confides the my nest,
(Men respect such a hideout,)

i pɔβrə i panruk
i pobre i panruch,
and poor and not clever,

əntrə lə fəmiljə baʃ də lə təːwlaðə
entre la familia, baix de la teulada,
between the family, small of the roof,
(my family lives in a small place,)

məmpərə kɔm puk
M'ampare com puch.
I shelter myself as I can.

ləs frujts dəl bɔsk buskə lə tɔrkək lə ɣriβə
Les fruits del bosch busca la torcac; la griva,
The fruits from the wood small piece the wood pidgeon, the partridge
(The wood pidgeon carries off the fruit from the orchard)

ʒəŋglɔts entrəls pampuls ləstruneʎ lə uliβə
Janglots entre'ls pampols; l'estornell, la oliva;
Bunches of grapes among the vine leaves; the starling, the owl;
(The partridge takes grapes from the vine;)

ə serps bərinɔsəs lus bistɔs fləmɛŋk
A serps verinoses, los vistós flamench;
To snakes poisonous, the spectacular flamingo;
(To poisonous snakes, the spectacular flamingo;)

lə ʎantiə ðəl templə lə uliβə furtiβə
La llántia del temple, la óliva furtiva,
The oil lamp of the temple, the owl furtive,
(The furtive owl desecrates the temple,)

i əɲeʎs ləβɔriβɔl kɔndur fəmulɛŋk
i anyells l'aborrívol condor famolench.
and lambs the bored condor starving.
(and the bored condor gobbles the lambs.)

ʒo bisk də ləlmɔjna kə əl umil maːj faʎa
Jo visc de l'almoyna que al humil mai falla;
I survive from the donations to the humble never fail
(I survive from the donations of crumbs)

i əm sənt benəstruk
I em sent benastruch;
I feel lucky;

lu grə kən ləs ərəs sə pərõ entrə paʎə
Lo grá qu'en les eres se perd entre palla,
The grain that in the lost threshing floor between the straw
(The grain that is lost between the straw in the threshing floor)

rəpləɣə kɔm puk
Replegue com puch.
I grab it up as I can.

Idiomatic translation:
Happy hunter, pursue more ferocious prey and leave me in peace. I am a friend of this house and I am just a sparrow. I am not as beautiful as the goldfinch with its beautiful, flashy colors; I lack the sweet voice of the nightingale; nor am I as nimble as the stork that can cross the sea with one flight. I dress plainly in gray, without flowers or stripes. I sing of my sadness and my joy. Although the eagles nest in cliffs and turtledoves live in tree roots, I, poor and not very smart, shelter myself as well as I can. The thrush robs fruit from the orchard and the starling eats grapes. The bored condor eats the lambs, but I survive from donations to the poor. I am lucky to eat the grain that is lost on the threshing floor between the straw, and I grab it as quickly as I can.

kantisil
2. Canticel
Song

pər unə bɛlə ən əl mar bla:w
Per una vela en el mar blau,
For a sail in the sea blue,
(To sail the blue sea,)

dariən sɛptrə
Daria un ceptre,
I would give a throne,

pər unə bɛlə ən əl mar bla:w
Per una vela en el mar blau,
For a sail in the sea blue,
(To sail the blue sea,)

septrə i palaːw
Ceptre i palau.
a throne and palace.

pər lalə ʎeːw duna birtut
Per l'ala lleu d'una virtut,
For to see the face of virtue,
(To see a virtuous face,)

mon gɔtʃ daria
Mon goig daria,
My joy I would give,
(I would give my joy,)

jəl trɔs kə em rrəstə mitʃ rromput
Y el tros que em resta mig romput
and the fragment that me left half broken
(and the half broken fragment left to me)

də ʒuβəntut
De juventut.
of youth.

pər unə flɔ də ruməni
Per una flor de romani,
For a flower of rosemary,
(For rosemary,)

ləmor dariə
L'amor daria,
My love I would give,
(I would give my love,)

pər unə flo də ruməni
Per una flor de romani,
For a flower of rosemary,
(For rosemary,)

ləmor duni
L'amor doni...
My love I give...

Idiomatic translation:
    For a sail on the high seas, I would give my throne and a palace.
To see a virtuous face, I would give my joy and a part of my youth.
For rosemary, I would give my love. For rosemary, I give my love.

liŋkiətut priməβerəl də lə dunzeʎə
3. L'Inquietut Primaveral de la Donzella
The Anxious Springtime of the Maid

arə buldrjə summərʒirmə tuðа
Ara voldria submergirme toda
Now I would like to submerge all
(Now I would like to completely submerge myself)

dintrə laːjrə də mar kəl kɔs pərfumə
Dintre l'aire de mar que el cos perfuma
Inside the air of the sea that the body perfumes
(Between the sea air that perfumes the body)

i ən laːjɣwə klara dunə pladʒə iŋnɔtə
I en l'aigua clara d'una platja ignota
and from there the water clear from a beach undiscovered
(And in the clear water of an undiscovered beach)

rriəʎəra dəl sɔl i flɔ dəskurna
Riallera del sol i flor d'escurna.
Laughing by the sun and flower of rammacies. (a type of flower)

dəspuəs biŋdriə ə ʒɛnrə pər lə praðə
Despues vindria a jenre per la prada
After I would come to show by the meadow
(Afterwards, I would come to the meadow to show)

ʃopə suptil lə kəβəʎərə boʒə
Xopa i subtil la cabellera boja:
Soaked and fine the hair wild:
(My wild, soaked hair)

sərkariə unə flɔ bεn əromaðə
Cercaria una flor ben aromada
Seek a flower very aromatic
(I would seek an aromatic flower)

pər fɔndrəiən un bɛs mə bokə rrɔʒə
Per fondrehien un bes ma boca roja.
To melt a kiss my mouth red.
(To kiss my red mouth.)

ənʒujariə dəspres mɔn kɔs də deə
Enjoiaria després mon cos de Dea
Adorn with jewels after my body of the Goddess Dea
(I would then adorn my body with jewels like the Goddess Dea)

ambrəmətyəs flurits də ləs fɔntənəs
Ambramatges florits de les fontanes,
Amber flowers of the fountains,

i ərraŋkəriə kɔrrə pəls kəmins
I arrancaria a córrer pel's camins.
And would start to run for his path.

əmbriɣəðə dəl sɔl də ləs kləriənəs
Embrigada del sol de les clarianes
Intoxicated from the sun of the mountains in Catabria

tɔt uint lə ʎuŋada məlɔpea
tot oint l'a llunyada melopea
all listen to the far away songs

dun fluβjɔl də sətir bɔsk endins
d'un fluviol de satir bosc endins.
of a river of satire inside the forest.

Idiomatic translation:
    I would like to drown myself in the sea air and bathe in the clear water of a hidden beach. Afterwards, I would enjoy the sun and flowers and seek a flower to kiss my mouth. Like the Goddess Dea, I would adorn my body with jewels. Intoxicated from the sun in the mountains in Catabria, I would listen to the songs sung by the river.

bruʎəðo ʒəntil
4. Brollador Gentil
Fountain Gentle

nit pərfums i kləro dɔlsə
Nit, perfums i claror dolça
Night, perfumes and brightness sweet
(Night, perfumes and sweet brightness)

rrəʒə laiɣwəl bruʎəðo
Raja l'aigue al brolladó
Flows the water from the fountain
(water flows from the fountain)

əl bɔn parə də lə molsə
El bon pare de la molsa
The good father of the moss

ba tukənt əl gitarrɔ
Va tocant el guitarró.
Goes playing the guitar.

ən lə pikə rrəɣələðə
En la pica regalada
In the peak dripping
(In the dripping peak)

kaðə nɔtəs ba əʃamplənt
Cada nota es va eixamplant
Each note is exemplary
(Each note grows bigger and bigger)

fins kəmor əmprəzunəðə
Fins que amor empresonada
Until that love is imprisoned
(Until love imprisons the notes)

pər ləs peðrəs dəl bultan
Per les pedres del voltant.
By the stones of the vicinity.
(By the surrounding stones.)

əʎ dəls truβəðo ɛs əl kəntaːjrə
Ell dels trobador és el cantaire,
He of the troubadors is the singing,
(The troubador is the singer,)

əl dəl rri:wrə sənitɑs
El del riure sanitós,
The of the laugh healthy,
(with the hearty laugh,)

əl kə tɔt puʒənt ən laːjrə
El que tot pujant en laire
the that here rises in the wind
(As it rises in the air)

ba turnənt sə ʎuminɑs
Va tornant-se lluminós.
He is becoming illuminated.

əl əs tota ələɣiə
Ell és tota l'alegria
He is all happiness

dəkɛʎ rrəpɔs bənɛit
D'aquell repós beneit,
Of that rest blessed,
(Of that blessed rest,)

si əl kəʎes əs muririə
Si ell callés es moriria
If he is silent it would be death

lu kə es ərə mes flurit
Lo que és ara més florit.
That what is now more flowered.

pətriarkə də bɛndərə
Patriarca de vendara
Patriarch of feudal times

mai sə sənt əl ʎaβi
Mai se sent el llavi
Never he feels his lip

pər ʃukantə əβuːj
Per xocanta avui encara
For surprising today still
(For still surprising today)

kɔm ən plənə ʒuβəntut
Com en plena joventut.
As in full youth.

Idiomatic translation:
   As water springs from the fountain, the night perfumes the sweet air. The father of the moss plays his guitar until love captures the notes by the surrounding stones. The troubadour sings and laughs as his notes fill the air. The singer is joyful and at peace with his luminous sound. If he were silent, he would die. Because he doesn't feel the passage of time, he still lives in his youth.

Notes

   1. Cecilia Rodrigo, E-mail to author, April 23, 1998.
   2. Philip Ward, ed., The Oxford *Companion to Spanish Literature* (Oxford: Clarendon Press, 1978), 332.
   3. C. Rodrigo, E-mail, April 23, 1998.
   4. Ward, *Oxford*, 97.

Chapter 8

Cuatro canciones sefardíes

kwatrɔ kansjɔnɛz sɛfarðiɛz

Cuatro canciones sefardíes	6:40
Four Sephardic Songs	
I. Respóndemos	2:10
II. Una pastora yo amí	1:15
III. Nani, nani	2:15
IV. "Morena" me llaman	1:00

Anonymous text, adapted by Victoria Kamhi
Vocal Range: D^4 to F^5
For medium voice and piano

This cycle holds special significance for Maestro Rodrigo because of Victoria's ethnicity. He wrote:

> Since my wife was born in Turkey and was of Sephardic origin, I have always been attracted to the music of Sephardic origin, since this culture forms part of Spanish tradition and cultural history, which is well known to me. I have also composed three songs for choir, based on Sephardic music. These are: "Dos canciones sefardíes del siglo XV"; "Malato está el hijo del rey, El rey que muncho madruga"; and "Triste estaba el rey David."[1]

157

The first song is dedicated to Isaac Kamhi, Victoria Kamhi's beloved father. The second song is dedicated to Professor M. J. Benardete. "Nani, nani" is dedicated to Pilar and Walter Rubin, good friends of the Rodrigos. Pilar is a painter and Walter served as the director of the Spanish program for the American base at Torrejón de Ardoz. He was later a professor of Spanish literature at the University of Houston.[2] "Morena me llaman" is dedicated to Isabel Penagos, a singer-friend whom Victoria accompanied. The cycle was premiered by Fedora Alemán in November 1965.[3]

rɛzspɔndɛmɔz
I. **Respóndemos**
Respond to Us

rɛspɔndɛmɔz di:ɔ ðɛ aβɾaham rɛspɔndɛmɔz
¡Respóndemos, Dio de Abraham, respóndemos!
Respond to us, God of Abraham, respond to us!

rɛspɔndɛmɔz ɛl kɛ rɛspɔndɛ ɛn la ɔɾa ðɛ vɔluntað
Respóndemos, el que respónde en la ora de voluntad.
Respond to us, he who responds in the hour of need.

rɛspɔndɛmɔz pavɔr ðɛ jitsxak rɛspɔndɛmɔz
¡Respóndemos, pavor de Yitshak, respóndemos!
Respond to us, terror of Isaac, respond to us!

rɛspɔndɛmɔz ɛl kɛ rɛspɔndɛ ɛn ɔɾa ðɛ aŋguztja
Respóndemos, el que respónde, en ora de angustia,
Respond to us, he who responds, in the hour of anguish,

rɛspɔndɛmɔz fwɛrtɛ ðɛ ja:kɔv rɛspɔndɛmɔz
¡Respóndemos. Fuerte de Yaakov, respóndemos!
Respond to us. Strong one of Yaakov, respond to us!

rɛspɔndɛmɔz di:ɔ ðɛ la mɛrkava rɛspɔndɛmɔz
Respóndemos. Dio de la merkava, Respóndemos.
Respond to us. God of the merkava (the chariot of fire that God sent to the prophet Elijah to ascend into heaven), respond to us.

rɛspɔndɛmɔz ɔ paðɾɛ piaðɔzɔ i ɣɾasjɔzɔ rɛspɔndɛmɔz
¡Respóndemos, o Padre piadoso y gracioso, respóndemos!
Respond to us, oh Father pious and merciful, respond to us!

Idiomatic translation:
    Respond to us, O God of Abraham, Isaac, and Jacob. Answer us in
our hour of need. You who responds in the hour of anguish, be
merciful to us.

una paztɔɾa jɔ ami
II. Una pastora yo amí
I Loved a Shepherdess

una paztɔɾa jɔ ami
Una pastora yo amí,
A shepherdess that I loved

una iʒa ɛrmɔza
una hija hermoza,
a daughter beautiful,
(a beautiful daughter,)

dɛ mi tʃikɛz kɛlaðɔɾi
de mi chiques quel'adori,
since my childhood I her adored,
(since my childhood I adored her,)

maz kɛja nɔ a mi
más qu'ella no a mí.
but she not love to me.
(but she did not love me.)

un di:a kɛ ɛztavamɔz
Un día que estavamos
One day that we were

ɛn la wɛrta azɛntaðɔz
en la huerta asentados,
in the garden sitting,
(sitting in the garden,)

lɛ ðiʃɛ jɔ pɔr ti mi flɔr
le dixe yo: "Por tí, mi flor,
I said to her: "For you, my flower,

mɛ mwɛɾɔ ðɛ amɔr
me muero de amor."
I die of love."

Idiomatic translation:
I loved a beautiful shepherdess since my childhood, but she didn't love me. One day when we were sitting in the garden, I said to her, "I could die because of my love for you, my beautiful flower."

nani nani
III. Nani, nani
Cradle Song

nani nani nani kɛɾɛl iʒɔ ðɛ la maðɾɛ
Nani, nani, nani, quere el hijo de la madre,
Nani, nani, nani, that the son of the mother,

dɛ tʃikɔ sɛ aɣa ɣɾandɛ
de chico se haga grande.
from small will do great things.
(even while young will do great things.)

aɾi aɾi durmitɛ mi alma
Ay, ay, dúrmite, mi alma,
Ay, ay, sleep, my soul,

durmitɛ mi viða
dúrmite, mi vida,
sleep, my life,

kɛ tu paðɾɛ vjɛnɛ kɔn mutʃalɛɣɾia
que tu padre viene con mucha alegría.
that your father comes with much happiness.

aɾj avɾimɛʃ la pwɛrta
Ay, avrimex la puerta,
Ay, open to me the door,
(Ay, open the door to me,)

avɾimɛʃ mi ðama
avrimex, mi dama,
open it, my madame,

kɛ vɛŋgɔ muj kanzaðɔ
que vengo muy cansado
that I come very tired

ðɛ aɾar laz wɛrtaz
de arar las huertas.
from ploughing the fields.

aːj la pwɛrta jɔ vɔz avɾɔ
Ay, la puerta yo vos avro,
Ay, the door I to you open,
(Oh, I will open the door to you,)

kɛ vɛniʃ kanzaðɔ
que venix cansado,
that you came tired,
(since you are so tired,)

i vɛɾɛʃ ðurmiðɔ al iʒɔ ɛn la kuna
y verex durmido al hijo en la cuna.
and you will see sleeping the boy in the cradle.

Idiomatic translation:
   This young boy, the son of his mother, will accomplish great things. Ay! Sleep, my soul and my life. Your father will greet you with joy. He says, "Open the door, Ma'am, for I am tired of ploughing the fields." "I'll open the door for you since you are tired and want to see the sleeping boy in the cradle."

mɔɾɛna mɛ jaman
IV. **"Morena" me llaman**
"Dark-Skinned Girl" They Call Me

mɔɾɛna mɛ jaman
"Morena" me llaman,
"Dark-skinned girl" they call me,

jɔ βlaŋka nasi
yo blanca nací.
I white was born.
(I was born white.)

dɛ pazɛar ɣalana
De pasear, galana,
From strolling, charming one,

mi kɔlɔr pɛrði
mi color perdí.
my color I lost.
(I lost my color.)

dɛ akɛjaz vɛntanikaz
De aquellas ventanicas
From those windows

marrɔnʒan flɛtʃaz
m'arronjan flechas;
to me are hurled arrows;
(arrows are hurled at me;)

si sɔn dɛ amɔɾɛz vɛŋgan
si son de amores, vengan,
if they are of love, let them come,

vɛŋgan dɛɾɛtʃaz
vengan derechas!
let them come to the right hands!

Idiomatic translation:
    People call me "the dark-skinned girl," but I was born pale. I became brown from strolling in the sun. From the windows, arrows are shot. If they are love's arrows, they have come to the right place!

Notes

    1. Cecilia Rodrigo, E-mail to author, April 23, 1998.
    2. Victoria Kamhi, *Hand in Hand with Joaquín Rodrigo, My Life at the Maestro's Side,* trans. Ellen Wilkerson (Pittsburgh: Latin

American Literary Review Press, 1992), 192.
  3. Kamhi, *Hand in Hand*, 221.

Chapter 9

Cuatro madrigales amatorios

kwatɾɔ maðɾiɣalɛs amatɔɾjɔs
Cuatro madrigales amatorios (1947)   7:00
Four Madrigales of Love

(Inspirados en musica española del siglo XVI)
(Inspired by Spanish music of the 16th century)

¿Con qué la lavaré?	2:00
Vos me matásteis	2:00
¿De dónde venís, amore?	1:00
De los álamos vengo, madre	2:00

Vocal range: F^4 to C^6 (high voice)
For voice (high or low) and piano or voice and orchestra

Orchestra: 2 flutes and piccolo, 2 oboes, 1 clarinet, 1 horn, 1 trumpet, triangle, strings

These songs were composed for voice and piano in 1947 and transcribed for voice and orchestra the following year.
    The four singers to whom these songs are dedicated, Blanca Maria Martínez Seoane, Celia Langa, María Angeles Morales, and Cármen Pérez Durias, were former pupils of Lola Rodriguez Aragón, a

prominent teacher in Spain in the 1940s, 1950s and 1960s. Ms. Aragón played a primary role in the postwar musical world of Spain as a teacher and a performer. Ms. Aragón opened her Advanced School of Song in Madrid in 1972, and her studio has produced many fine singers, including Teresa Berganza. Cármen Pérez Durias, to whom the fourth song is dedicated, was often accompanied by Maestro Rodrigo in concerts. All four singers had brilliant careers in the 1950s and 1960s.[1]

This cycle is well known and much loved due to its exquisite poetry, lovely text settings, and diversity of accompaniment. All four songs are love poems and are included in a collection of poetry entitled *Recopilacion de sonetos y sonatos y villancicos a quatro y a cinco* (1560). In this collection, Juan Vasquez (c. 1510-1560) included his poetry as well as other popular poetry of the day.[2]

Rodrigo, true to Baroque style, suggests terraced dynamics in these songs, with few crescendi. The chord structures and rhythms are simple and typical of Baroque Spanish folk music. The last song of the cycle, "De los álamos vengo, madre," is flamboyant in its use of guitar rasgueado strumming patterns.

kɔŋ kɛ la laβaɾɛ
1. **¿Con qué la lavaré?**
With What It Shall I Wash?
(With What Shall I Wash?)

kɔŋ kɛ la laβaɾɛ
¿Con qué la lavaré?
With what it shall I wash?
(With what shall I wash?)

la tɛθ ðɛ la mi kaɾa
la tez de la mi cara?
the skin of my face?

kɔŋ kɛ la laβaɾɛ
¿Con qué la lavaré?
With what it shall I wash?
(With what shall I wash?)

kɛ βiβɔ mal pɛnaða
que vivo mal penada?
that I live badly punished?

laβansɛ las kasaðas
Lávanse las casadas
They wash the married women

kɔn aɣwa ðɛ limɔnɛs
con agua de limones.
with water from lemons.

laβɔmɛ jɔ kwitaða
Lavome yo, cuitada,
I wash myself, anguished,

kɔm pɛnas i ðɔlɔɾɛs
con penas y dolores.
with grief and sorrow.

Idiomatic translation:
    With what shall I bathe myself? The wives and mothers bathe
with lemon water. I will wash my marks of anguish with tears wrung
from my sorrow.

bɔz mɛ matastɛjs
2. Vos me matásteis
You Me Killed
(You Killed Me)

bɔz mɛ matastɛjs
Vos me matásteis,
You me killed,
(You killed me,)

niɲa ɛŋ kaβeʎɔ
niña en cabello,
girl with the hair,

bɔz mɛ aβejz mwɛrtɔ
vos me habéis muerto.
you me have killed.
(you have killed me.)

riβɛɾaz ðɛ un riɔ
Riberas de un río,
Riverbank of a river,
(At the river's edge,)

bi mɔθa βirxɛn
ví moza vírgen,
I saw girl virgin,
(I saw a virgin,)

niɲa ɛŋ kaβɛʎɔ
niña en cabello,
girl with the hair,

bɔz mɛ aβejz mwɛrtɔ
vos me habéis muerto.
you me have killed.
(you have killed me.)

Idiomatic translation:
        You have destroyed me, girl with the beautiful hair. You have killed me. On the banks of the river, I saw you. You have killed me with your love.

        This poem depicts a young maiden with her beautiful, long hair and an observer. The girl is "killing him" with her eyes, a theme common in Spanish verse.[3]

dɛ ðɔndɛ βɛnis amɔɾɛ
3. ¿De dónde venís, amore?
From where you come, love?
(From where do you come, love?)

dɛ ðɔndɛ βɛnis amɔɾɛ
¿De dónde venís, amore?
From where you come, love?
(From where do you come, love?)

bjɛn sɛ jɔ ðɛ ðɔndɛ
bien sé yo de donde.
Well know I from where.
(I know well from where.)

dɛ ðɔndɛ βenis amiγɔ
¿De dónde venís, amigo?
From where you come, friend,
(From where do you come, friend?)

fwɛɾɛ jɔ tɛstiγɔ
Fuere yo testigo. Ah!
Have been I a witness. Ah!
(I have been a witness. Ah!)

Idiomatic translation:
    Where have you been, my beloved? I know well where you have
been. Where have you been, my friend? I have been a witness. Ah!

dɛ lɔs alamɔz βeŋgɔ maðɾɛ
4. De los álamos vengo, madre
From the poplars I come, mother

dɛ lɔs alamɔz βeŋgɔ maðɾɛ
De los álamos vengo, madre,
From the poplars I come, mother,

dɛ βɛr kɔmɔ lɔz mɛnɛa ɛl ajɾɛ
de ver cómo los menea el aire.
to see how they move in the air.

dɛ lɔs alamɔz ðɛ sɛβiʎa
De los álamos de Sevilla,
From the poplars of Seville,

dɛ βɛr a mi linda amiγa
de ver a mi linda amiga.
to see my pretty girlfriend.

Idiomatic translation:
    I have been by the poplars, mother. I have seen their branches
swaying in the breezes. Ah! I have seen my beautiful lover by the
poplar trees of Seville.

Notes

1. Tina Sandor Bunce, "Joaquín Rodrigo's *Cuatro madrigales*

amatorios," Bowling Green State University Master's Thesis. (August 1985), 11.

2. Cecilia Rodrigo, E-mail to author, April 23, 1998.

3. Bunce, *Cuatro madrigales amatorios*, 16.

Chapter 10

Doce canciones españolas

dɔθɛ kanθjɔnɛs ɛspaɲɔlas

Doce canciones españolas (1951)	19:25
Twelve Spanish Songs	
1. ¡Viva la novia y el novio!	:40
2. De ronda	:50
3. Una Palomita blanca	1:15
4. Canción de baile con pandero	:45
5. Porque toco el pandero	:50
6. Tararán	7:00
7. En las montañas de Asturias	:50
8. Estando yo en mi majada	:40
9. Adela	1:55
10. En Jerez de la Frontera	1:20
11. San José y Maria	1:20
12. Canción de cuna	2:00

Vocal Range: C^4 to G-flat ^{5}

For voice and piano

Doce canciones españolas was premiered on March 3, 1952, at the Atheneum in Madrid with Marimí del Pozo, soprano, and Victoria Kamhi, pianist. The cycle is dedicated to Marimí del Pozo, a well known soprano of the 1950s and 1960s, who is currently living and teaching in Madrid. Ms. Pozo premiered the orchestral version of *Cuatro madrigales amatorios* in the United States, and, because she sang the world premiere of *Doce canciones*, Maestro Rodrigo dedicated the cycle to her.[1] When the cycle was recorded in October of that year, Victoria accompanied eight of the songs, and Joaquín accompanied the remaining four.[2]

The poetry *Doce canciones españolas* is from the great cancioneros, or song books, that flourished during the fifteenth, sixteenth, and seventeenth centuries. These cancioneros, some of which include hundreds of poems, contain poetry by well-known poets of the day, but also many anonymous works. The earliest collection, the Cancionero of Baena, dates from the mid-fifteenth century and was compiled in honor of John the Second. It contains 576 poems, some in the Galician dialect, but most are in Castilian. There are fifty or so poets represented, and the poetic tone is light and in a popular style.

In 1511, the "Cancionero General" was printed in Valencia. It included

> many and diverse works of all or of the most notable Troubadours of Spain, the ancient as well as the modern, in devotion, in immortality, in love, in jests, ballads, villancicos, songs, devices, mottoes, glosses, questions, and answers.[3]

There are eleven hundred and fifteen poems in this collection.

Between 1514 and 1573, nine additional "Cancioneros Generales" were printed, which included the works of hundreds of poets; thousands of poems. Some of the poems are regarded as delightful, whereas others are crude and mediocre.

Although it is impossible to date the poems Rodrigo set in this cycle, the poems are typical of the Renaissance Cancioneros. The texts he selected are lyrical *canciones*, or songs intended by their creators to be sung. These poems are often love songs, free in form and in order of rhyme, offering the listener great variety and charm. The texts represent various provinces in Spain.

biβa la nɔβja i ɛl nɔβjɔ
1. ¡Viva la novia y el novio!
Long Live the Bride and the Groom!
from Puerta Lapice (León)

bɪβa la nɔβja jɛl nɔβjɔ jɛl kuɾa kɛ lɔs kasɔ
¡Viva la novia y el novio y el cura que los casó,
Long live the bride and the groom and the priest who them marries,

jɛl paðɾinɔj la maðɾina lɔs kɔmbiðaðɔs i jɔ
y el padrino y la madrina, los convidados y yo!
and the godfather and the godmother, the wedding guests and I!

bɪβa la nɔβja jɛl nɔβjɔ i la maðɾɛ kɛ lɔs paɾjɔ
¡Viva la novia y el novio y la madre que los parió,
Long live the bride and the groom and the mother who them birthed,

jɛl paðɾinɔj la maðɾina lɔs kɔmbiðaðɔs i jɔ
y el padrino y la madrina, los convidados y yo!
and the godfather and the godmother, the wedding guests and I!

Idiomatic translation:
    Long live the bride, and the groom, and the priest who marries them. Long live the bride and the groom, and the mother who gave them birth, the godfather and the godmother, the wedding guests and me!

dɛ rɔnda
2. De ronda
The Round
from León

manθanita kɔlɔɾaða
Manzanita colorada,
Little apple red,
(Little red apple,)

kɔmɔ nɔ tɛ kaɛs al swɛlɔ
¿como no te caes al suelo?
why not you fall to the ground?
(why don't you fall to the ground?)

tɔða la βiðaɛ andaðɔ la rɛsalaða
¡Toda la vida he andado, la resalada,
All the life I have walked, charming one,
(All my life, charming one, I have walked,)

pɔr alkanθartɛj nɔ pwɛðɔ
por alcanzarte y no puedo!
to reach you and I cannot!

dɛntɾɔ ðɛ mi pɛtʃɔ tɛŋgɔ
Dentro de mi pecho tengo
Inside of my heart I keep

dɔs ɛskalɛɾaz ðɛ βiðɾjɔ
dos escaleras de vidrio;
two ladders of glass;

pɔr una suβɛl kɛɾɛr la ɾɛsalaða
Por una sube el querer, la resalada
On one climbs the love, charming one

pɔr ɔtɾa βaxa ɛl kaɾiɲɔ
Por otra baja el cariño.
On the other falls the affection.

Idiomatic translation:
    Little red apple, how is it that you don't fall to the ground? All my life, I have been walking around, charming one, and I am not able to reach you. Inside my heart, I keep two glass ladders. Love climbs one, charming one, while affection flies down the other.

una palɔmita βlaŋka
3. Una Palomita blanca
A Dove White
(A White Dove)
from León

una palɔmita βlaŋka
Una palomita blanca
A dove white
(a white dove)

kɔmɔ la njɛβɛ
como la nieve,
like the snow,

baxal riɔ a βɛβɛr aɣwa
baja al río a beber agua,
comes to the river to drink water,

baɲarsɛ kjɛɾɛ
bañarse quiere.
to bathe it wishes.
(it wishes to bathe.)

palɔma si βas al mɔntɛ
Paloma, si vas al monte,
Dove, if you go to the mountain,

miɾa kɛ sɔj kaθaðɔr
mira que soy cazador.
understand that I am a hunter.

si tiɾɔ un tiɾɔj tɛ matɔ
Si tiro un tiro y te mato,
If I shoot a shot and you I kill,
(If I fire a shot and kill you,)

paɾa ti sɛɾa ɛl dɔlɔr
para tí será el dolor,
for you it will be the sadness,
(it will be sad for you,)

palɔma βlaŋka kɔmɔ la njɛβɛ
paloma blanca como la nieve.
dove white like the snow.
(dove as white as the snow.)

Idiomatic translation:
    A little white dove falls to the river to drink and bathe. Little dove, if you go to the mountain, remember that I am a hunter. If I were to shoot and kill you, it would be sad for you, little white dove.

kanθɔn dɛ βajlɛ kɔm pandɛɾɔ
4. Canción de baile con pandero
Song of the Tambourine Dance
from León

ɛn ɛl mar aj um pɛskaðɔ
En el mar, hay un pescado,
In the sea, there is a fish,

kɛ tjɛnɛ las puntaz βɛrðɛs
que tiene las puntas verdes,
that has the points green,
(that has green points,)

ɛn ɛstɛ pwɛβlɔ aj um mɔθɔ
en este pueblo hay un mozo,
in this town there is a young man,

kɛ tɔðaz laz mɔθas kjɛɾɛ
que todas las mozas quiere.
who all the young girls he wants.
(who wants all the young girls.)

ɛn ɛl riɔ ɛn ɛl riɔ laβandɔ
En el río en el río, lavando,
In the river, in the river, washing,

ɛn ɛl riɔ mɛa ðitʃɔ un sɔldaðɔ
en el río, me ha dicho un soldado;
in the river, to me has said a soldier;
(a soldier said to me;)

si kjɛɾɛz βɛnir kɔmmiɣɔ
Si quieres venir conmigo,
If you want to come with me,

tɛ mɔntaɾɛm mi kaβaʎɔ
te montaré en mi caballo.
you I'll mount on my horse,
(I'll mount you on my horse,)

jɔ lɛ ðixɛ ni kjɛɾɔ ni pwɛðɔ
Yo le dije: ni quiero ni puedo,
I to him said: I don't wish to nor can I,

kɛ sɔj niɲa ðɛ amɔɾɛz nɔ ɛntjɛndɔ
que soy niña, de amores no entiendo.
that I am a girl, of loves not I understand.
(I am a girl, I don't understand about love.)

Idiomatic translation:
There is a fish in the sea with green fins. In this town, there is a young man who has all the young girls he wishes. I was washing in the river when a soldier said to me: If you want to come with me, I'll mount you on my horse. I told him that I don't want to and that I cannot. I'm just a girl and I don't understand about love.

pɔrkɛ tɔkɔ ɛl pandɛɾɔ
5. Porque toco el pandero
Because I Play the Tambourine
from León

pɔrkɛ tɔkɔ ɛl pandɛɾɔ mi maðɾɛ riɲɛ
Porque toco el pandero, mi madre riñe,
Because I play the tambourine, my mother quarrels,

pɔrkɛ rɔmpɔ xustiʎɔ mandil i ðɛŋgɛ
porque rompo justillo, mandil y dengue.
because I tear my waist, apron and affectation.

bɛn a βɛrmɛ manwɛl dɛl alma
Ven a verme, Manuel del alma,
You come to see me, Manuel of my soul,

bɛn a βɛrmɛ kɛ sɔj tu ðama
Ven a verme, que soy tu dama.
You come to see me, that I am your woman.

ɛm mɛðjɔ ðɛ la plaθa ɛm mɛðjɔ mɛðjɔ
En medio de la plaza, en medio, medio,
In the middle of the town square, in the middle, middle,

aj una ɛnɾɛðaðɛɾa dɔndɛ mɛn rɛðɔ
Hay una enredadera donde me en redo.
There is an entanglement where I am caught.

bɛn a βɛrmɛ manwɛl dɛl alma
Ven a verme, Manuel del alma,
You come to see me, Manuel of my soul,

bɛn a βɛrmɛ kɛ sɔj tu ðama
ven a verme, que soy tu dama.
You come to see me, I am your woman.

Idiomatic translation:
When I play the tambourine, my mother complains that I am tearing my skirts. In the middle of the town square, there is an entanglement that catches me and won't let me go. Come see me, Manuel of my soul. I am your lover.

taɾaɾan
6. **Tararán**
Tararán
from Cuenca

taɾaɾan si βjɛs a la una
Tararán, si viés a la una,
Tararán, if you come at one,

bɛɾas ɛl niɲɔ ɛn la kuna
verás el Niño en la cuna,
you will see the Boy in the cradle.

(Refrain)
jɛl βɛlɛn ɛn ɛl pɔrtal
Y el Belén en el portal,
And Bethlehem in the entrance,

kɛ nɔ aj taɾaɾan
que no hay, tararán,
that there is no one, tararán,

kɔmɔ aðɔɾar al niɲɔ
como adorar al Niño,
like to adore the Christ Child,
(like the Christ Child to adore,)

kɛ nɔ aj taɾaɾan
que no hay, tararán,
that there is no one, tararán,

kɔmɔ al niɲɔ aðɔɾar
como al Niñõ adorar.
like the Christ Child to adore.

taɾaɾan si βjɛs a laz ðɔs
Tararán, si viés a las dos,
Tararán, if you come at two,

bɛɾas al ixɔ ðɛ ðjɔs
verás al hijo de Dios.
you will see the son of God.

taɾaɾan si βjɛs a las tɾɛs
Tararán, si viés a las tres,
Tararán, if you come at three,

bɛɾas al niɲɔtɾa βɛθ
verás al Niño otra vez.
you will see the Boy again.

taɾaɾan si βjɛs a las kwatɾɔ
Tararán, si viés a las cuatro,
Tararán, if you come at four,

bɛɾas al niɲɔ ɛn ɛl kwartɔ
verás al Niño en el cuarto.
you will see the Boy in the room.

taɾaɾan si βjɛs a las θiŋkɔ
Tararán, si viés a las cinco,
Tararán, if you come at five,

daɾas al niɲɔ um bɛsikɔ
darás al Niño un besico.
you will give the Boy a kiss.

taɾaɾan si βjɛs a las sɛjs
Tararán, si viés a las seis,
Tararán, if you come at six,

beɾas la mulaj ɛl βwɛj
verás la mula y el buey.
you will see the mule and the ox.

taɾaɾan si βjɛs a las sjɛtɛ
Tararán, si viés a las siete,
Tararán, if you come at seven,

tɾaɛɾas al niɲɔ un rɔʎɛtɛ
traerás al Niño un rollete.
you will bring the Boy a roll.

taɾaɾan si βjɛs a las ɔtʃɔ
Tararán, si viés a las ocho,
Tararán, if you come at eight,

tɾaɛɾas al niɲɔ um biθkɔtʃɔ
traerás al Niño un bizcocho.
you will bring the Boy a small cake.

taɾaɾan si βjɛs a laz nwɛβɛ
Tararán, si viés a las nueve,
Tararán, if you come at nine,

ɛmpina la βɔtaj βɛβɛ
empina la bota y bebe.
raise the wineskin and drink.

taɾaɾan si βjɛs a laz ðiɛθ
Tararán, si viés a las diez,
Tararán, if you come at ten,

bwɛlβɛ a βɛβɛr ɔtɾa βɛθ
vuelve a beber otra vez.
he returns to drink another time.

taɾaɾan si βjɛs a las ɔnθɛ
Tararán, si viés a las once,
Tararán, if you come at eleven,

bɛɾas al ni ɲɔ ðɛ βɾɔnθɛ
véras al Niño de bronce.
you will see the Boy of bronze.

taɾaɾan si βjɛs a laz ðɔθɛ
Tararán, si viés a las doce,
Tararán, if you come at twelve,

dilɛ al ni ɲɔ kɛ rɛtɔθɛ
dile al Niño que retoce.
tell the Boy to frolic.

Idiomatic translation:
Tararán, if you come at one, you'll see the Boy in the cradle. If you come at two, you'll see the Son of God. If you come at three, you'll see the Boy another time. If you come at four, you'll see the Boy at the door. If you come at five, you'll give the Boy a little kiss. If you come at six, you'll see the mule and ox. If you come at seven, you'll bring the Boy a roll. If you come at eight, you'll bring the Boy a small cake. If you come at nine, you'll raise the bottle and drink. If you come at ten, you'll return to drink another time. If you come at eleven, you'll see the Boy of bronze. If you come at twelve, tell the Boy to frolic. Come adore the Holy One in Bethlehem.

ɛn laz mɔntaɲaz ðɛ astuɾjas
7. En las montañas de Asturias
In the Mountains of Asturias
from Cuenca

ɛn laz mɔntaɲaz ðɛ astuɾjas
En las montañas de Asturias
In the mountains of Asturias

unastuɾjana βi
una asturiana ví,
an Asturian girl I saw,
(I saw an Asturian girl,)

dɛ katɔrθɛ a kinθɛ aɲɔs
de catorce a quince años,
of fourteen or fifteen years,

rɛɣandɔ su xarδin
regando su jardín.
watering her garden.

pasɔ uŋ kaβaʎɛɾɔ
Pasó un caballero,
Passed by a horseman,
(A horseman passed by,)

lɛ piδɛ una flɔr
le pide una flor,
he asked for a flower,

i la βɛʎastuɾjana lɛ δiθɛ kɛ nɔ
y la bella asturiana le que dice no.
and the pretty Asturian girl him told no.
(and the pretty Asturian girl told him no.)

kɛδa kɔn djɔs astuɾjana
Queda con dios, asturiana,
Stay with God, Asturian girl,

mɛ la tjɛs kɛ paɣar
me la tiés que pagar;
me you must pay;
(you must pay me;)

pɔr la kwɛstjɔn dɛ una flɔr
por la cuestión de una flor,
for the question of a flower,

tɛ tɛŋgɔ kɛ matar
te tengo que matar.
you I have to kill.
(I have to kill you.)

Idiomatic translation:
    In the hills of Asturias, I saw a country girl, fourteen or fifteen

years old, watering her garden. A caballero passed by and asked her for a flower, but the pretty country girl answered no. "Go with God, girl. You must pay for your answer. Because you answered no, I must kill you."

This *serranilla*, like the *canciones* and *villancicos*, combines a folk feeling with refined delicacy and grace. Poems of this type are known for their simplicity and freshness as well as for their exquisiteness of expression. The serranillas often describe the encounter of a gentleman with a rustic girl, who when propositioned may respond with either a "yes" or a "no."

εstandɔ jɔ εm mi maxaða

8. **Estando yo en mi majada**
I Was Guarding My Sheep
from Cáceres

εstandɔ jɔ εm mi maxaða
Estando yo en mi majada,
Being I in my sheepfold,
(I was guarding my sheep,)

mε martʃε paɾa laldεa
me marché para l'aldea,
I left for the village,

a βεr la fjε̃ta ðεl kɔrpu
a ver la fiehta del Corpuh,
to see the fair of Corpus,

kε ðiθεn kε kɔsa βwεna
que dicen qu'eh cosa buena.
that they say is a good thing.

aj βa βɔmba βa
Ay, va, bomba, va,
Oh, go, bass drum, go,

kε ðεl kɔrpu la jamam mɔɾεna
que del Corpuh la yaman morena.
that the Corpus calls her dark haired girl

kɛ ðɛl kɔrpu la jaman
Que del Corpuh la yaman
That the Corpus calls her

pɔr kɔsa θjɛrta
por cosa cierta,
for certain,

aj βa βɔmba βa
ay va, bomba, va!
Oh, go, bass drum, go!

Idiomatic translation:
When I was in my sheepfold, I walked to the village to see the Corpus Christi fair. Everyone says it is a wonderful thing! Play, bass drum, play! The fiesta calls to the dark haired girl. It calls her for certain. Play, bass drum, play!

aðɛla
9. Adela
Adela
from Granada

una mutʃatʃa ɣwapa ʎamaðaðɛla
Una muchacha guapa llamada Adela,
A maid handsome called Adela,
(A handsome maid called Adela,)

lɔs amɔɾɛz ðɛ xwan la ʎɛβa ɛɲfɛrma
los amores de Juan la lleva enferma,
the love of Juan has made her sick,

jɛʎa saβia jɛʎa saβia
y ella sabía y ella sabía,
and she knew and she knew,

kɛ su amiɣa ðɔlɔɾɛz lɔ ɛntrɛtɛnia
que su amiga Dolores lo entretenía.
that her girlfriend Dolores him amused.
(that her girlfriend Dolores amused him.)

ɛl tjɛmpɔ iβa pasandɔ i la pɔβɾɛ aõɛla
El tiempo iba pasando, y la pobre Adela,
The time passed and the poor Adela,

maz βlaŋka sɛ pɔnia i mas ɛɲfɛrma
mas blanca se ponía y más enferma,
more white she became and more sick,

jɛʎa saβia kɛ õɛ sus amɔɾɛs sɛ mɔɾiɾia
y ella sabía, que de sus amores se moriría.
and she knew, that of love she would die.

Idiomatic translation:
A handsome girl named Adela was in love with Juan. Her love for him made her sick. She knew that her friend Dolores was entertaining him. Time passed and poor Adela grew more ill. She knew that she would die because of her love for Juan.

ɛn xɛɾɛθ õɛ la frɔntɛɾa
10. **En Jerez de la Frontera**
In Jerez of the Frontier
from Ciudad Real

ɛn xɛɾɛθ õɛ la frɔntɛɾa
En Jerez de la Frontera
In Jerez of the Frontier

aβia um mɔlinɛɾɔnɾaõɔ
había un molinero honrado,
lived a miller honored,
(lived an honored miller,)

kɛ ɣanaβa su sustɛntɔ
que ganaba su sustento
who was earning his sustenance

kɔn um mɔlinɔ alkilaõɔ
con un molino alquilado.
with a mill rented.
(with a rented mill.)

pɛɾɔ ɛs kasaðɔ kɔn una mɔθa
Pero es casado con una moza
But he is married to a girl

kɔmɔ una rɔsa
como una rosa,
like a rose,

kɔmɔ ɛs tam bɛ‎ʎa
como es tan bella,
as she is so pretty,

ɛl kɔrrɛxiðɔr nwɛβɔ
el corregidor nuevo
the mayor new
(the new major)

pɾɛndɔ ðɛʎa
prendó d'ella.
desired her.

ɛn xɛɾɛθ ðɛ la frɔntɛɾa
En Jerez de la Frontera,
In Jerez of the Frontier

riɛsɛ la mɔlinɛɾa
ríese la molinera,
laughed the miller's wife,
(the miller's wife laughed,)

jal kɔrrɛxiðɔr ðɛθia
y al corregidor decía,
and to the mayor said,
(and said to the mayor,)

kɛ amɔɾɛz lɛ pɛðia
que amores le pedía:
that love he requested of her:

aj sɔjs ɣɾaθjɔsɔ
"Ay, sois gracioso,
Oh, you are humorous,

muj ẋenɛɾɔsɔ
muy generoso,
very generous,

muj lisɔnẋɛɾɔ
muy lisonjero,
very flattering,

tambjɛn kaβaʎɛɾɔ
también caballero.
also a gentleman.

mas kjɛɾɔ a mi molinɛɾɔ
Mas quiero a mi molinero,
But I want my miller,

ɛz mi ðwɛɲɔ
es mi dueño."
he is my master."

Idiomatic translation:
   In Jerez of the Frontier lived an honest miller. He rented a mill in which to grind the corn. His wife was as pretty as a rose, and the new mayor was smitten with her. The miller's wife made merry, and when the mayor attempted to win her she said, "You are humorous, generous, flattering and quite a gentleman, but I want my miller. He owns my heart."

san xɔsɛ i maɾia
11. **San José y Maria**
Saint Joseph and Mary
from Badajoz

san xɔsɛj maɾia βan pɔr tjɛrra santa
San José y Maria van por Tierra Santa,
Saint Joseph and Mary go to Land Holy,

a kumplir la lɛj kɛl θɛsar lɛ manda
a cumplir la ley qu'el César leh manda.
to fulfill the law that the Caesar ordered.

pwɛ kɔn sɛr lɔ rɛjɛ ðɛ θjɛlɔ i tjɛrra
Pueh con ser lo Reyeh de cieloh y tierrah,
Thus with being the King of heaven and earth,

a kumplir la lɛj ɣutɔsɔ sɛ prɛtan
a cumplir la ley guhtosoh se prehtan.
to fulfill the law with pleasure.

pɔr ɛtɔ nɔ ðiθɛn kɛ a lautɔɾiða
Por ehto noh dicen que a l'autoridá
For this they say that to the authority

grandɛ i pɛkɛɲɔ suxɛtɔ ɛtan
grandeh y pequeñoh sujetoh ehtán.
the grand and small are subject.

Idiomatic translation:
Saint Joseph and Mary go to the Holy Land to fulfill the law of the Caesar. Even though they are with the King of heaven and earth, they fulfill the law. For this reason, great and small people must also obey the authority.

This poem is in the dialect of Badajoz, with added aspirate hs. It is still pronounced in the Castilian manner.[4]

kanθjɔn dɛ kuna
12. Canción de cuna
Cradle Song
from Ciudad Real

ɛn tu pwɛrta tɛɾɛsa kanta uŋ kanaɾjɔ
En tu puerta, Teresa, canta un canario,
By your door, Teresa, sings a canary,

ɛtʃalɛ kaɲamɔnɛs kɛ kantɛ klarɔ
échale cañamones que cante claro.
throw birdseed so that he sings clearly.

kambru kambru sɛɾɛnaðɔ sɛɾɛnaðitɔ kambru
Cambrú, Cambrú, serenado, serenadito, Cambrú,
Cambrú, Cambrú keep quiet, Cambrú, serenading, Cambrú,
(the boy's name is Cambrú)

kɛ a lɔs pjɛz ðɛ la kama ʎɔɾa ɛl niɲɔ ðɛ la u
que a los pies de la cama llora el niño de la U,
that at the foot of the bed crying the boy of the U,
(the boy of the U is crying at the foot of the bed,)

i su maðɾɛ lɛ ðiθɛ ɛa baja
y su madre le dice: ea, vaya,
and his mother to him says: I rock you,

kaʎa nɔ ʎɔɾɛs kɛ βjɛnɛl βu
calla, no llores, que viene el bú,
be quiet, don't cry, that comes the Bogeyman,

sɛɾɛnaðitɔ kambru
serenadito, Cambrú.
serenading, Cambrú.

al arruʎɔ al arruʎɔ dwɛrmɛ mi niɲɔ
Al arrullo, al arrullo, duerme mi niño;
By means of cooing, cooing, sleeps my son;

dwɛrmɛ mi niɲɔ dwɛrmɛ dwɛrmɛ al arruʎɔ
duerme mi niño, duerme, duerme al arrullo.
sleeps my boy, sleep, sleep to the cooing.

Idiomatic translation:
A canary sings outside your door, Teresa. Throw him some birdseed so that he'll sing brightly. I lull my baby to sleep. Sleep well, my baby. Rou-cou, rou-cou, serenading, sing to the crying little boy at the foot of the bed, and his mother says: "Quiet, don't cry or the Bogeyman will get you."

"Canción de cuna" is steeped in folklore with its images of the "Bogeyman" and the "little boy crying at the end of the bed." One doesn't usually consider these figures soporific, but they do appear in other Spanish cradle songs.

Notes

1. Cecilia Rodrigo, E-mail to author, April 23, 1998.

2. Victoria Kamhi, *Hand in Hand with Joaquín Rodrigo, My Life at the Maestro's Side,* trans. Ellen Wilkerson (Pittsburgh: Latin American Literary Review Press, 1992), 152.

3. George Ticknor, *History of Spanish Literature,* 6th ed. 3 vols. (New York: Gordian Press, Inc., 1965), 457.

4. Cecilia Rodrigo, interview with author, July 27, 1998.

Chapter 11

Dos canciones para cantar a los niños

dɔs kanθjɔnɛs paɾa kantaɾ a lɔz niɲɔs

Dos canciones para cantar a los niños (1973)	5:45
Two Songs to Sing to the Children	
Corderito Blanco	3:00
Quedito	2:45

Vocal Range: D^4 to $F^{\#5}$
For medium voice and piano

These charming songs are dedicated to Maestro Rodrigo's grand-daughter, Pati. Both songs are settings of anonymous poetry adapted by Victoria Kamhi.

kɔɾðɛɾitɔ βlaŋkɔ
I. **Corderito Blanco**
Little Lamb White
(Little White Lamb)

kɔrðɛɾitɔ βlaŋkɔ
Corderito blanco
Little lamb white
(Little white lamb)

kɛ ðurmjɛndɔ ɛstas
que durmiendo estás,
that sleeping-you are,
(that is sleeping,)

dɛxatɛ βjɛm miɔ,
déjate, bien mío,
let yourself, well mine,
(let yourself, sweet one,)

ðɛxatɛ arruʎar
déjate arrullar.
let yourself be cooed to sleep.

si tɛ ðwɛrmɛs amɔr miɔ
Si te duermes, amor mío,
If you sleep, love mine,
(If you sleep, my love,)

jɔ tɛ kjɛɾɔ ðɛspɛrtar
Yo te quiero despertar,
I you wish to awaken,
(I wish you to awaken,)

pwɛz βinjɛɾon dɛzðɛ ɔɾjɛntɛ
pues vinieron desde Oriente
since they came from the Orient
(since from the Orient)

lɔs tɾɛz rɛjɛs aðɔɾar
los tres Reyes a adorar.
the three Kings to adore.
(the three Kings came to adore you.)

nɔ tɛ ŏwɛrmaz mi βiŏa
No te duermas, mi vida:
No you sleep, my life:
(Don't you fall asleep, my life:)

nɔ tɛ ŏwɛrmaz mi θjɛlɔ
No te duermas, mi cielo:
No you sleep, my heaven:
(Don't you fall asleep, my heaven:)

arrɔrrɔ arrɔrrɔ
Arrorró; arrorró,
Lullaby, lullaby,

kɛ tɛ arruʎɔ jɔ
que te arrullo yo.
that you lull to sleep I.
(I will lull you to sleep.)

Idiomatic translation:
    You are a little white lamb sleeping there. My baby, let me lull
you to sleep. But if you sleep, my love, I may wish to awaken you
since the Three Kings came from the Orient to adore you. Don't fall
asleep, my life, my love. I will lull you to sleep.

kɛŏitɔ
II. Quedito
Very Quietly

kɛŏitɔ pasitɔ
Quedito, pasito,
Very quietly, softly,

silɛnθjɔ tʃitɔn
silencio, chitón,
silence, hush,

kɛ ŏwɛrmɛ un iɱfantɛ
Que duerme un infante,
That sleeps a child,
(that a child may sleep,)

kɛ tjɛrnɔj kɔnstantɛ
que tierno y constante,
who tender and constant,

al mas tiβjɔ amantɛ
al más tibio amante
to the more warm lover
(to the warmest lover)

dɛspjɛrtal kalɔr
despierta al calor.
he awakens to the heat.

nɔ lɛ ðɛspjɛrtɛn nɔ
No le despierten, no;
No him wake, no;
(Don't wake him, no;)

a la ɛ a la ɔ
a la e_____ a la o_____,
a la e_____ a la o_____,

nɔ lɛ ðɛspjɛrtɛn nɔ
no le despierten, no.
no him wake, no.
(don't wake him, no.)

dwɛrmɛ mjamaðɔ
¡Duerme, mi amado,
Sleep, my dear,

ðɛskansa mjamɔr
descansa, mi amor!
he rests, my love!

Idiomatic translation:
   Be very quiet. Softly, silence, hush, so that a child may sleep.
While he is constantly and tenderly cared for, he will awaken to the
warmth of my love. Don't awaken him, no. Sleep, my dear. Rest, my
love.

Chapter 12

Dos poemas

dɔs pɔɛmas

Dos poemas	4:50
Two Poems	
Verde verderol	3:00
Pájaro del agua	1:50

Vocal Range: B^3 to F^5
For medium voice and flute

These two songs, "Verde verderol" and "Pájaro del agua," are settings of poetry by Juan Ramón Jiménez. The French translation, by Victoria Kamhi, is included in both the Ediciones Joaquín Rodrigo and Union Musical Ediciones editions. "Verde verderol" is dedicated to the world-renown singer Teresa Berganza, and "Pájaro del agua" is dedicated to Fedora Alemán. Alemán, the excellent Venezuelan singer, performed frequently with Maestro Rodrigo at the piano. She sang the world premier of *La Grotte* in France.[1]

These songs exemplify Maestro Rodrigo's fascination with birds. He loves bird song, uses it often in his orchestral music, and sets poems praising birds.[2]

Juan Ramón Jiménez (1881-1958), born in Huelva, is known as one of Spain's most influential modern lyric poets. Although he was not part of any poetic school, he was an important link between Darís and the Generation of 1927. His poetry gradually evolved from symbolism and modernism to his own unique style, one that he termed "poesía desnuda."[3] He rejected florid writing and wrote in an intelligent style, known for its haunting beauty and caressing sonority. Themes included loneliness, sorrow, and the mystery of human existence. Jiménez was awarded the Nobel Prize for Literature in 1956. His poetry is printed in two major collections--*Segunda antolojía poética*, which included 522 poems, and *Tercera antolojía*, containing 720 poems.[4]

bɛɾδɛ βɛɾδɛɾɔl
Verde, Verderol
Green, Greenfinch

bɛɾδɛ βɛɾδɛɾɔl
Verde, verderol
Green, greenfinch,

ɛndulθa la pwɛsta δɛl sɔl
¡endulza la puesta del sol!
sweeten the setting of the sun!

palaθjɔ δɛŋkantɔ
Palacio de encanto,
Palace of enchantment,

ɛl pinar tarδiɔ
el pinar tardío
the pine tree was late

arruʎa kɔn ʎantɔ
arrulla con llanto
lull to sleep with weeping
(being lulled to sleep with weeping)

la wiδa δɛl riɔ
la huida del río.
the flight of the river.

aʎi ɛl niðɔ umbɾiɔ
Allí el nido umbrío
There the nest shady
(There the shady nest)

tjɛnɛl βɛɾðɛɾɔl
tiene el verderol.
holds the greenfinch.

bɛɾðɛ βɛɾðɛɾɔl
Verde verderol
Green greenfinch

ɛndulθa la pwɛsta ðɛl sɔl
¡endulza la puesta del sol!
sweeten the setting of the sun!

la ultima βɾisa
La última brisa
The last breeze

ɛs suspiɾaðɔɾa
es suspiradora,
is sighed,

ɛl sɔl rɔxɔ jɾisa
el sol rojo irisa
the sun red is iridescent
(the red sun is iridescent)

al pinɔ kɛ ʎɔɾa
al pino que llora.
to the pine that weeps.

baɣaj lɛnta ɔɾa
¡Vaga y lenta hora
Lazy and sluggish hour

nwɛstɾa bɛɾðɛɾɔl
nuestra, Verderol!
our, greenfinch!

bɛɾ́ðɛ βɛɾ́ðɛɾɔl
Verde verderol
Green greenfinch,

ɛndulθa la pwɛsta ðɛl sɔl
¡endulza la puesta del sol!
sweeten the setting of the sun!

sɔlɛðað i kalma
Soledad y calma,
Solitude and calm,

silɛnθjɔj ɣɾandɛθa
silencio y grandeza.
silence and magnificence.

la tʃɔθa ðɛl alma
La choza del alma
The hut of the soul

sɛ ɾɛkɔxɛj ɾɛθa
se recoge y reza.
itself gathers and prays.
(gathers itself and prays)

dɛ pɾɔntɔ ɔ βɛʎɛθa
De pronto ¡oh belleza!
From quickly, oh beauty!

kanta ɛl βɛɾ́ðɛɾɔl
canta el verderol.
sings the greenfinch.

su kantɔ ɛnaxɛna
Su canto enajena.
Her song intoxicates.

sɛ a paɾaðɔ ɛl βjɛntɔ
(¿Se ha parado el viento?)
(It has motionless the wind?)
(Has the wind stopped?)

εl kampɔ sε ʎɛna
El campo se llena
The countryside fills up

ðε su sεntimjεntɔ
de su sentimiento.
from her emotion.

malβa εs εl lamεntɔ
Malva es el lamento,
Mauve is the lament,

bεɾðεl βεɾðεɾɔl
verde el verderol.
green is the greenfinch.

bεɾðε βεɾðεɾɔl
Verde verderol
Green greenfinch,

εndulθa la pwεsta ðεl sɔl
¡endulza la puesta del sol!
sweeten the setting of the sun!

Idiomatic translation:
    Greenfinch, with your song, sweeten the setting of the sun. In the enchanting woods, the pine tree could not sleep because it was crying over the flight of the river. The greenfinch is in its shady nest. As the sun sets, the last breeze is sighed and the pine weeps. This is our lazy and sluggish hour, greenfinch! Our souls pray in the silent, calm magnificence. The greenfinch sings her intoxicating song. Has the wind stopped? The countryside is filled with emotion as it listens to the bird's lament. Green greenfinch, sweeten the setting of the sun!

paxaɾɔ ðεl aɣwa
Pájaro del agua
Bird of the Water

paxaɾɔ ðεl aɣwa
¡Pájaro del agua!
Bird of the water!

kɛ kantas kɛŋkantas
¿Qué cantas, que encantas?
What do you sing, that you enchant?

a la tarðɛ nwɛβa
A la tarde nueva
To the afternoon new
(to the new afternoon)

ðas una nɔstalxja
das una nostalgia
you give a nostalgia

ðɛtɛrniðað fɾɛska
de eternidad fresca,
of eternity fresh,
(of fresh eternity)

ðɛ ɣlɔɾja mɔxaða
de gloria mojada.
of glory moist.
(of moist glory)

ɛl sɔl sɛ ðɛznuða
El sol se desnuda
The sun itself bares
(The sun bares itself)

sɔβɾɛ tu kantata
sobre tu cantata.
over your cantata.

paxaɾɔ ðɛl aɣwa
¡Pájaro del agua!
Bird of the water!

dɛzðɛ lɔz rɔsalɛz
Desde los rosales
From the rosebushes

ŏɛ mi xarŏin klama
de mi jardin clama
of my garden it cries out

a ɛsaz nuβɛz βɛʎas
a esas nubes bellas
to those clouds beautiful
(to those beautiful clouds)

karɣaŏaz ŏɛ laɣɾimas
cargadas de lágrimas.
burdened by tears.

kisjɛɾa ɛn laz rɔsas
Quisiera en las rosas
I wanted in the roses

βɛr ɣɔtaz ŏɛ plata
ver gotas de plata.
to see drops of silver.

paxaɾɔ ŏɛl aɣwa
¡Pájaro del agua!
Bird of the water!

mi kantɔ tambjɛn
Mi canto también
My song also

ɛs kantɔ ŏɛ aɣwa
es canto de agua.
is the song of water.

ɛm mi pɾimaβɛɾa
En mi primavera
In my springtime

la nuβɛ ɣɾiz βaxa
la nube gris baja
the cloud gray falls
(the gray cloud falls)

asta lɔz rɔsalɛz
hasta los rosales
to the rosebushes

ðɛ mis ɛspɛranθas
de mis esperanzas.
of my hopes.

paxarɔ ðɛl aɣwa
¡Pájaro del agua!
Bird of water!

amɔ ɛl sɔl ɛrrantɛ
Amo el sol errante
I love the sun wandering
(I love the wandering sun)

jaθul kɛ ðɛzɣranas
y azul que desgranas
and blue that you shake loose

ɛn las ɔxaz βɛrðɛs
en las hojas verdes,
in the leaves green,
(in the green leaves,)

ɛn la fwɛntɛ βlaŋka
en la fuente blanca.
in the fountain white.
(in the white fountain.)

nɔ tɛ βajas tu
¡No te vayas tú!
No you go you!
(Don't leave!)

kɔraθɔŋ kɔn alas
Corazón con alas.
Heart with wings.

paxaɾɔ ŏɛl aɣwa
¡Pájaro del agua!
Bird of water!

kɛ kantas kɛŋkantas
¿Qué cantas, que encantas?
What do you sing, that you enchant?

Idiomatic translation:
Bird of the water, how can your song be so enchanting? To the new afternoon, you give a nostalgia of fresh eternity, of moist glory. The sun bares itself over your cantata. Bird of water! From the roses in my garden, your song cries out to the beautiful clouds heavy with tears. I wanted to see silver drops in the roses. My song is also the song of water. In my springtime, the gray cloud falls to the rosebushes of my hopes. I love the wandering sun and the blue that you shake loose in the green leaves and in the white fountain. Don't leave, heart with wings! Bird of water, how can your song be so enchanting?

Notes

1. Cecilia Rodrigo, E-mail to author, April 23, 1998.
2. C. Rodrigo, interview with author, July 27, 1998.
3. Philip Ward, ed. The Oxford *Companion to Spanish Literature* (Oxford: Clarendon Press, 1978), 301.
4. Jelena Krstovíc, ed., *Hispanic Literature Criticism*, vol.1 Detroit: Gale Research Inc., 1994), 730.

Chapter 13

La grotte

la grɔt

La grotte (1962)   3:45
The Cave

Louis Emié, poet
Vocal range: $C^{\#}4$ to G^5
For voice and piano

The poet, Louis Emié, wrote this text to commemorate the one hundredth anniversary of Claude Debussy's birth. The songs were commissioned by the Bordeaux May Musical and were premiered at that festival in the spring of 1962 by the Venezuelan soprano Fedora Alemán and Victoria Kamhi, pianist.[1]

Louis Emié (1900-1967) was a minor French poet, novelist, and essayist. He worked as a journalist, editing a daily newspaper, *Sud Ouest*, and he knew and corresponded with the literary giants of his time--Max Jacob, Jean Cocteau, Jean Rostand, and others. He published only two novels, *La Nuit d'octobre* (1929) and *Le Dieu sans tête* (1944). He often composed verse, and then encouraged by his friend Henri Sauguet, he set it to music. Emié's best poetic works include *Amour de notre amour* (1939), *L'Ange* (1958), and *Coplas* (1965). Because his mother was Spanish, he considered Spain his motherland and wrote impassioned, sensual essays and verse to express his affection for his adopted country.[2]

la grɔt

I. La grotte
The Cave

dɑ sɛt grɔt u lə silɑ̃:s
Dans cette grotte où le silence
In this cave where the silence

iɲɔrɑ̃kɔːr kil nu fɛ pœr
ignore encor qu'il nous fait peur,
ignores still that it us is afraid,
(ignores that it is afraid of us,)

jekutə lə kœːr də tɔ̃ kœːr
j'écoute le coeur de ton coeur
I hear the heart of your heart

dɑ̃ le zɔ̃:brə kil nu dispɑ̃:s
dans les ombres qu'il nous dispense.
in the shadows that it to us bestows.

le zɔ̃:brə nɔ̃ kœ̃ sœl viza:ʒ
Les ombres n'ont qu'un seul visage
The shadows only have a single face

e ty la ʃwazi puːr kœ̃ juːr
et tu l'as choisi pour qu'un jour
and you it chose for only one day
(and you chose it for only one day)

il swa ply fidɛla lamuːr
il soit plus fidèle á l'amour
it is more faithful to love

kə twa mɛːma mɔ̃ peiza:ʒə
que toi-même à mon paysage.
than you yourself to my home.

amuːr dã sɛt grɔt ɔpskyːr
Amour, dans cette grotte obscure
Love, in this cave obscure

u nu zatãdɔ̃ za ʒənu
où nous attendons à genoux
where we wait on our knees

nə saprɔʃəra pwẽ də nu
ne s'approchera point de nous
will not approach ever of us
(will not approach us)

sil nɛ nɔ trɔ̃ːbrə la ply pyrə
s'il n'est notre ombre la plus pure.
if it isn't our shadow the most pure.
(if it isn't our purest shadow.)

Idiomatic translation:
    In this quiet cave, I can hear the depths of your heart. The shadows
have only a single face, but they are more faithful to love than you are
to me. Love will not come near to us, as we wait here on our knees, if
our shadows are not pure.

II.

kɛl ɛ sɛt ɔ̃ːbrə ki makabl
Quelle est cette ombre qui m'accable
What is this shadow that overwhelms me

dã sɛt grɔt u ʒə tatã
dans cette grotte où je t'attends,
in this cave where I you await,
(in this cave where I wait for you,)

u la ply bɛl flœːr dy tã
où la plus belle fleur du temps
where the most beautiful flower of time

nɛ ʒamɛ kə rɑːz də saːbl
n'est jamais que rose de sable?
is nothing but a rose of sand?

sɛt ɔ̃ːbrə dɔ̃ tɔ̃ nɔ̃ːbrɛ fɛtə
Cette ombre dont ton ombre est faite
This shadow of which your shadow is made

flɔt syr de zo ki sɑ̃ vɔ̃
flotte sur des eaux qui s'en vont
floats on the waters that go

o dəla dœ̃ sjɛl si prɔfɔ̃
au delà d'un ciel si profond
beyond a heaven so deep

kil nə ʃarmə kœ̃ kɔːr sɑ̃ tɛt
qu'il ne charme qu'un corps sans tête.
that it charms only a body without judgment.

ty nɛ də ʃɛːr e də vizaːʒ
Tu n'es de chair et de visage
You aren't of flesh and of face

kə paːr lɔ̃ːbrə ki meblwi
que par l'ombre qui m'éblouit,
that by the shadow who me dazzles,
(that by the shadow that dazzles me,)

rɑːz də saːbl kə la nɥi
rose de sable que la nuit,
rose of sand that the night,

roː zɑ̃kɔːr divi ze partaʒə
rose encor, divise et partage.
pink still, divides and shares.

Idiomatic translation:
    What is this shadow in this cave that overwhelms me as I wait for
you, where the most beautiful flower is nothing but a rose of sand?
This shadow, of which your shadow is made, floats on the water that

goes beyond a heaven so deep that it charms only a mindless body. You are not made of flesh, for the shadow that fascinates me, rose of sand that the night, still pink, divides and shares.

III.

si ʒegzi stãkɔːr sur la tɛːr
Si j'existe encor sur la terre
If I exist still on the earth

u le zɔ̃ːbrə negzistə pa
où les ombres n'existent pas
where the shadows don't exist

sɛ kə mɔ̃ nɔːbrə aːtrə te bra
c'est que mon ombre, entre tes bras,
it is that my shadow, between your arms,

sə fɛ ʃɛːr dœ̃ nɔːtr mistɛːrə
se fait chair d'un autre mystère.
pretends to be flesh of another mystery.

dã sɛt grɔte sə myrmyːrə
Dans cette grotte et ce murmure,
In this cave and this murmur,

ki nu ʃɛrʃ puːr sekute
qui nous cherche pour s'écouter
that we search for ourselves to hear,
(that we search to hear ourselves,)

mɔ̃ nɔːbrə dwatɛl dute
mon ombre doit-elle douter
my shadow must it doubt
(that my shadow must doubt)

də sɛl ki la trãsfigyrə
de celle qui la transfigure?
of that one who is transfigured?
(that which transfigures it?)

amuːr nɛ ty dɔ̃k kœ̃ vizaːʒ
Amour, n'es tu donc qu'un visage
Love, are you only a face

dɔ̃ le zjø nə sɔ̃ kə mezjø
dont les yeux ne sont que mes yeux
in which the eyes are only my eyes

dɑ̃ sɛt grɔt u ʒə nə vø
dans cette grotte où je ne veux
in this cave where I do not wish

mə vwaːr ka travɛːr tɔ̃ nimaʒə
me voir qu'à travers ton image.
myself to see except through your image?
(to see myself except through your image?)

Idiomatic translation:
If I still exist on this earth, where shadows don't exist, it is because my shadow in your arms, gives flesh to another mystery. In this cave, where we indulge ourselves in whispers, my shadow must doubt that which transfigures it? Love, are you only a face in which your eyes are only my eyes in this cave, where I do not wish to see myself except through your image?

Notes

1. Victoria Kamhi, *Hand in Hand with Joaquín Rodrigo, My Life at the Maestro's Side,* trans. Ellen Wilkerson (Pittsburgh: Latin American Literary Review Press, 1992), 203.

2. Louis Emié, *Dialogues avec Max Jacob/Louis Emié : postface par Christine van Rogger Andreucci* (Bordeaux: Le Festin, 1994), iii.

Chapter 14

Líricas castellanas

lirikas kastɛʎanas

Líricas castellanas (1980)	5:55
Castilian Lyrics	
San Juan y Pascua	2:00
Despedida y soledad	2:30
Espera del amada	1:25

Vocal Range: B^3 to G^5
For soprano, flauta de pico (flute), corneto de madera (oboe), and vihuela (guitar)

This set of three songs was composed for soprano and antique instruments, but modern instruments may be used, as indicated in the score. The first performance of *Líricas castellanas* occurred at in the Carlos III Theater at El Escorial, the palace built by Felipe II between 1563 and 1584. Ana Higueras, soprano, premiered the work, with Queen Sofia and Princess Irene in attendance.[1]

This lovely cycle was written at the suggestion of Nancy Knowles, the sister of James Knowles, the great sculptor. James Knowles created a wonderful bronze bust of Maestro Rodrigo between 1980 and 1982, and thus the association between the Knowles and the Rodrigos began. Nancy Knowles performed with a group of musicians called

"Trio Live Oak," specializing in early music. The instrumentation and style of *Líricas castellanas* reflect the late Middle Ages and Renaissance periods. Queen Sofía of Spain expressed the desire to have Maestro Rodrigo dedicate a work to her, and, of course, the composer happily fulfilled her wish.[2]

san xwan i paskwa
San Juan y Pascua
Saint John and Easter

kɛ nɔ kɔxɛɾɛ βɛrβɛna
Que no cogeré verbena
That no I will take verbena
(that I will not take verbena)
(a type of plant with spikes or clusters of red, white, or purplish flowers)

ɛn la maɲana ðɛ san xwan
en la mañana de San Juan,
in the morning of Saint John,

pwɛz mis amɔɾɛs sɛ βan
pues mis amores se ván.
since my loves are gone.

kɛ nɔ kɔxɛɾɛ klaβɛlɛs
Que no cogeré claveles,
That no I will take carnations,
(That I will not take carnations,)

maðɾɛsɛlβa ni miɾaβɛlɛs
madreselva ni miraveles,
honeysuckle nor sunflowers,

sinɔ pɛnas taŋ kɾuɛlɛs
sino penas tan crueles
rather griefs so cruel

kwal xamas sɛ kɔxɛɾan
cual jamás se cogerán,
that never they will be taken,
(that they will never be taken,)

pwɛz mis amɔɾɛs sɛ βan
pues mis amores se ván.
since my loves they will be gone.
(since my loves will be gone.)

Idiomatic translation:
On the morning of St. John, I will not take verbena, carnations, honeysuckle, or sunflowers because my loves have left me. My grief is so cruel, it will never depart from me, since my loves are gone.

dɛspɛðiða i sɔlɛðað
Despedida y soledad
Farewell and solitude

bansɛ mis amɔɾɛs maðɾɛ
Vanse mis amores, madre,
They go my loves, mother,
(My loves, they go, mother,)

lwɛŋgas tjɛrraz βam mɔɾar
luengas tierras van morar,
to far away lands they go to dwell,

jɔ nɔ lɔs pwɛðɔlβiðar
yo no los puedo olvidar.
I not them I am able to forget.
(I cannot forget them.)

kjɛm mɛ lɔs aɾa tɔrnar
¿Quién me los hará tornar?
Who to me them will make return?
(Who will make them return to me?)

jɔ sɔɲaɾa maðɾɛ un swɛɲɔ
Yo soñara, madre, un sueño,
I may dream, mother, a dream,

kɛ mɛ ðiʃ nɛl kɔɾaθon
que me dix nel corazón,
that to me tells from the heart,
(that tells me from the heart,)

kɛ sɛ iβan lɔz mis amɔɾɛs
que se iban los mis amores
that they went them my loves
(that my loves go)

a las izlaz ðɛ la mar
a las islas de la mar.
to the islands of the sea.

kjɛm mɛ lɔs aɾa tɔrnar
¿Quién me los hará tornar?
Who to me them will make return?
(Who will make them return to me?)

jɔ sɔɲaɾa maðɾɛ un swɛɲɔ
Yo soñara, madre, un sueño,
I may dream, mother, a dream,

kɛ mɛ ðiʃ nɛl kɔɾaθɔn
que me dix nel corazón,
that to me tells from the heart,
(that tells me from the heart,)

kɛ sɛ iβan lɔz mis amɔɾɛs
que se iban los mis amores
that they went them my loves
(that my loves go)

a las tjɛrraz ðɛ aɾayɔn
a las tierras de Aragón.
to the lands of Aragon.

aʎa sɛ βan a mɔɾar
Allá se ván a morar,
There they go to stay,

jɔ nɔ lɔs pwɛðɔlβiðar
yo no los puedo olvidar.
I not them can forget.
(I cannot forget them.)

kjɛm mɛ lɔs aɾa tɔrnar
¿Quién me los hará tornar?
Who to me them will make return?
(Who will make them return to me?)

Idiomatic translation:
My loves have gone to far away lands, mother, and I am not able to forget them. Who will make them return to me? In my dreams, mother, I dream that my loves go to sea islands. Who will make them return to me? My heart tells me in my dreams that my loves go to Aragón to live. I am not able to forget them. Who will make them return to me?

ɛspɛɾa ðɛl amaðɔ
Espera del amado
Hope of the Beloved

al alβa βɛniz βwɛn amiɣɔ
Al alba venís, buen amigo,
At the dawn you come, good friend,

al alβa βɛnis
al alba venís.
at the dawn you come.

amiɣɔ ɛl kɛ jɔ mas kɛɾia
Amigo el que yo más quería,
Friend he that I most loved,
(the friend that I most loved,)

bɛnið al alβa ðɛl dia
venid al alba del día.
come at the dawn of the day.

amiɣɔ ɛl kɛ jɔ mas amaβa
Amigo el que yo más amaba,
Friend he that I most loved,
(the friend that I most loved,)

bɛnið a la luz ðɛl alβa
venid a la luz del alba.
come at the light of the dawn.

bɛnið a la luz ðɛl dia
Venid a la luz del día,
Come at the light of day,

nɔn trajajs kɔmpaɲia
non trayais compañía.
not bring company.
(do not bring company.)

bɛnið a la luz ðɛl alβa
Venid a la luz del alba,
Come at the light of dawn,

nɔn trajajs ɣraŋ kɔmpaɲia
non trayais gran compañía.
not bring grand company.
(bring little company.)

Idiomatic translation:
Come at the dawn, good friend. The friend that I loved most, come at the dawn. Come at the light of dawn and don't bring company.

Notes

1. Victoria Kamhi, *Hand in Hand with Joaquin Rodrigo, My Life at the Maestro's Side,* trans. Ellen Wilkerson (Pittsburgh: Latin American Literary Review Press, 1992), 303.
2. Cecilia Rodrigo, E-mail to author, September 10, 1998.

Chapter 15

Rosaliana

rosaljana

Rosaliana (1965)	9:45
Cuatro canciones sobre poemas de Rosalía de Castro	
Four songs on poems of Rosalía de Castro	
Cantart'ei Galicia	2:45
¿Por qué?	2:00
Adiós ríos, adiós fontes	3:30
¡Vamos bebendo!	1:30

Vocal Range: C^4 to A^5

For soprano and orchestra
Piano reduction by Claus-Dieter Ludwig

Orchestra: flute, oboe, B-flat clarinet, horn, tamburo piccoli, violins I and II, violas, celli, double basses

    This cycle was first performed on July 26, 1965, by Ana Higueras, to whom the cycle is dedicated, and the Municipal Orchestra of Galicia. The songs, on poems of Rosalía de Castro, were commissioned by the city council. The title, *Rosaliana*, is derived from Rosalía's first name.[1]

217

Rosalía de Castro (1837-1885), born in Santiago de Compostela, was a poet and novelist who wrote in both Castilian and Galician. In 1863, she published *A mi madre* in Castilian and *Cantares gallegos*, which was so popular in style that many of the poems became part of the folk song heritage, although they were original poems. *Follas novas* (1880) was followed by her masterpiece, *En las orillas del Sar* in 1884.[2] She is considered the major Spanish language poet in the second half of the nineteenth century, because modern Galician literature is born and culminates with her work. Themes include love of home-land, lost love, and resignation in the face of the cruelty of humanity. When Rosalía de Castro died of uterine cancer in 1885, she was mourned by the Galician people as a folk hero.[3]

kantartɛːj galiθja
1. Cantart'ei, Galicia
I Must Sing to You, Galicia

kantartɛːj galiθja
Cantart'ei, Galicia,
I must sing to you, Galicia

teːus ŏɔθɛs kantarɛs
teus doçes cantares,
your sweet songs,

kasi mo pɛðirɔn
qu'así mô pediron
that as such they asked me

na βejɾa ŏɔ maɾɛ
na veira do mare.
on the shores of the sea.

kantartɛːj galiθja
Cantart'ei, Galicia,
I must sing to you, Galicia,

na lɛŋgwa ɣalɛɣa
na lengua gallega,
in the Galician language,

konswɛlɔ ðɔz malɛs
consuelo dos males,
consoles the pains,

aliβjɔ ðas pɛnas
alivio das penas.
alleviates the sorrows.

mimɔsa sɔaβɛ
Mimosa, soave,
soft, sweet,

sɛntiða kɛʃɔsa
sentida, queixosa;
feeling, fussy;

ɛŋkanta si ri:ɛ
encanta si ríe,
enchants if she laughs,

kɔmmɔβɛ si tʃɔɾa
conmove si chora.
moves if she cries.

kal ɛla niŋguna
Cal ela, ningunha
Like her, there is no one

tan dɔθɛ kɛ kantɛ
tan doçe que cante
so sweet as she sings

sɔ:jðaðɛs amaɾyas
soidades amargas,
bitter solitudes,

sɔspiɾɔs amantɛs
sospiros amantes.
loving sighs.

mistɛrjuz ða tarðɛ
Misterious da tarde,
Mysteries of the afternoon,

murmuʃɔz ða nɔjtɛ
murmuxos da noite:
murmurs of the night:

kantartɛ:j galiθja
cantart'ei, Galicia,
I must sing to you, Galicia,

na βɛjɾa ðas fɔntɛs
na veira das fontes.
next to the fountains.

kasi mɔ pɛðiɾɔn
Qu' así mô pediron,
In this way they asked me,

kasi mɔ mandaɾɔn
qu' así mô mandaron,
in this way they demanded,

kɛ kantɛ kɛ kantɛ
que cant'e que cant'e,
that I sing, that I sing,

na lɛngwa kɛu falɔ
na lengua qu'eu falo.
in the language that I speak.

Idiomatic translation:
 I must sing to you, Galicia. I must sing in my native language to console my pain. There is no one who sings as sweetly as Galicia, enchanting all with her songs and moving them with her tears. Mysteries of the afternoon, murmurs of the night, sing to Galicia. I must sing in Galician, my native tongue.

pɔr kɛ
2. ¿Por qué?
Why?

pɔr kɛ miɲalmiɲa
¿Por qué, miña almiña
Why, my beloved

pɔr kɔra nɔn kɛɾɛs
por qu' hora non queres
why do you now not love

ɔ kɛ antɛs kɛri:as
o que antes querías?
he whom before you loved?
(the one you used to love?)

pɔr kɛ pɛnsamɛntɔ
¿Por qué, pensamento,
Why, thought,

pɔr kɔra nɔn βiβɛs
por qu'hora non vives
why do you not live

ɛamantɛz ðɛsɛjɔs
e'amantes deseyos?
and to loves listen?
(and not listen to your loves?)

pɔr kɛ mɛu ɛspɾitɔ
¿Por qué, meu esprito,
Why, my spirit,

pɔr kɔra tumildas
por qu'hora te humildas,
why do you humble yourself

kandɛɾas altiβɔ
cand'eras altivo?
when you used to be proud?

pɔr kɛ kɔraθɔn
¿Por qué, corazón,
Why, heart,

pɔr kɔɾa nɔn falas
por qu'hora non falas
why do you now not speak

falaɾɛs damɔr
falares d'amor?
words of love?

pɔr kɛ ʃa nɑn βatɛs
¿Por qué xa non bates
Why do you no longer beat

kɔn dɔθɛ βatiðɔ
con doce batido
with sweet rhythm

kɛ kalma ɔs pɛsaɾɛs
que calma os pesares?
that calms your sorrows?

pɔr kɛ ɛn fin djɔz mɛu
¿Por qué, en fin, Dios meu,
Why, finally, God my,
(Why, finally, my God,)

a un tɛmpɔ mɛ faltan
a un tempo me faltan
at this time to me I lack
(at this time do I lack)

a tɛrra jɔ θɛɔ
á terra y `o ceo?
earth and heaven?

ɔ ti rɔʃa ɛstrɛla
¡Ou ti, roxa estrela
Where you, bright star
(Where, bright star)

kɛ ðin kɛ kɔmiɣɔ
que din que comigo
that they say that with me

naθitʃɛ pɔjŏɛɾas
naciche, poideras
you were born, you will be able to

pɔr sɛmpɾɛ apaɣartɛ
por sempre apagarte,
for always you will shut off
(turn off forever)

ʃa kɛ nɔn puŏetʃɛ
xa que non pudeche
since that not you were able
(since you were not able)

pɔr sɛmpɾɛ alumarmɛ
por sempre alumarme!...
to always illuminate me!....

Idiomatic translation:
Why, my beloved, do you not love the one you loved before?
Why, thought, do you not live and listen to your loves? Why, my
spirit, why are you humble when you used to be proud? Why, heart,
why don't you speak words of love? Why don't you calm your
sorrows with the sweet rhythm of your beating heart? And finally,
why, my God, do I lack heaven and earth? Why were the stars not
able to illuminate me?

aŏjɔs riɔs aŏjɔs fɔntɛs
3. Adiós ríos, adiós fontes
Good-bye rivers, good-bye fountains

aŏjɔs riɔs aŏjɔs fɔntɛs
Adiós ríos, adiós fontes,
Good-bye rivers, good-bye fountains

aŏjɔs rɛɣatɔs pɛkɛnɔs
adiós regatos pequenos
good-bye little creek

aŏjɔs βista ŏɔz mɛus aʎɔs
adiós vista dos meus allos,
good-bye sight of my eyes,

nɔn sɛj kandɔ nɔz βɛɾɛmɔs
non sei cándo nos veremos.
not I know when we will see each other again.
(I do not know when we will see each other again.)

miɲa tɛrra miɲa tɛrra
Miña terra, miña terra,
My land, my earth,

tɛrra ðɔndɛ mɛu kɾiɛj
terra donde m'eu criey
land where I grew up

ɔrtiɲa kɛ kɛɾɔ tantɔ
hortiña que quero tanto,
little vegetable garden that I love so much,

fiɣɛɾiɲas kɛ pɾan tɛj
figueriñas que pran tey.
little fig trees that I planted.

pɾaðɔz riɔs arβɔɾɛðas
Prados, ríos, arboredas,
Meadows, rivers, groves,

pinaɾɛs kɛ mɔβɛ ɔ βɛntɔ
pinares que move ó vento
pine trees that move by the wind

paʃaɾiɲɔs pjaðɔɾɛs
paxariños piadores,
little birds chirping,

kasiɲa ðɛ mɛu kɔntɛntɔ
casiña de meu contento.
home of my content.

muiɲɔ ðɔs kastaɲaɾɛs
Muhiño d'os castañares,
Forest of chestnuts,

nɔjtɛs kɾaɾaz ðɛ luar
noites craras de luar,
nights clear with moonlight,

kampaniɲas timbɾaðɔɾaz
campaniñas timbradoras
little bells ringing
(little ringing bells)

ðа igɾɛsiɲa ðɔ luɣar
dá igresiña dó lugar.
of church of the town.
(of the town church.)

amɔɾiɲaz ðas silβɛjɾas
Amoriñas d'ás silveiras
Little blackberries among the brambles

kɛu ʎɛ ðaβɔ mɛu amɔr
qu'eu lle dab'ó meu amor,
that to them I used to give my love
(that I used to love)

kaminiɲɔs antɾɔ miʎɔ
caminiños antr'ó millo,
rows between the corn,

aðjɔs paɾa sɛmpraðjɔs
¡adiós para sempr'adiós!
good-bye forever, good-bye!

aðjɔs ɣɾɔɾja aðjɔs kɔntɛntɔ
¡Adiós gloria! !Adiós contento!
Good-bye glory! Good-bye happiness!

dɛjʃɔ a kasa ɔndɛ naθin
¡Deixo á casa onde nacin
I leave the house where I was born

dɛjʃɔ alðɛa kɛ kɔnɔθɔ
deixo áldea que conoço
I leave the village that I know

pɔr un mɔndɔ kɛ nɔn βin
por un mondo que non vin!
for a world never seen!

dɛjʃɔ amiyɔs pɔr ɛʃtɾaɲɔs
Deixo amigos por extraños,
I leave my friends for foreigners,

dɛjʃɔ a βɛjɣa pɔlɔ mar
deixo á veiga pó-lo mar,
I leave the valley for the sea,

dɛjʃɔ ɛn fin kantɔ βɛn kɛɾɔ
deixo, en fin, canto ben quero...
I leave, finally, all I love...

kɛ puðɛɾa nɔn dɛjʃar
¡Que pudera non deixar!...
That I could never leave behind!...

Idiomatic translation:
Good-bye rivers, fountains, creeks, and all that I so dearly love. I don't know when I will return. Good-bye my land, my earth, the place of my birth, my vegetable garden, the fig trees I planted. I will miss the meadows, rivers, groves, pines swaying in the wind, chirping birds, chestnut trees, moonlit nights, and little ringing bells of the town church. Little blackberries that I used to love, corn rows, good-bye forever. Good-bye happiness! Good-bye house where I was born. Good-bye village that I know. I am leaving for an unseen and unknown world. I leave my friends for strangers, I leave the valley for the sea and I leave behind all that I love. I wish I didn't have to leave!

bamɔz βeβɛndɔ
4. ¡Vamos bebendo!
Let's Go Drinking!

tɛɲɔ tɾɛs pitaz βɾaŋkas
Teño tres pitas brancas
I have three hens white
(I have three white hens)

ɛ un γalɔ nɛγɾɔ
e un galo negro,
and a cock black,
(and a black cock,)

kɛan dɛ pɔɲɛr βɔs ɔβɔs
que han de poñer bôs hovos,
that they will lay many eggs,

andandɔ tɛmpɔ
andand' ò tempo.
passage of time.
(with the passage of time.)

jɛi ðɛ βɛndɛlɔs kaɾɔs
Y hei de vendel-os caros
I will sell them expensive
(I will sell them at a high price)

pɔlɔ ʃanɛjɾo
pol-o Xaneiro,
in the month of January

jɛi ðɛ ʃuntalɔs kartɔs
y hei de xuntal-os cartos
and I will get enough money

paɾa un mantɛlɔ
para un mantelo,
for a long veil,

jɛjnɔ ðɛ lɛβar pɔstɔ
y heino de levar posto
and I will wear

nɔ kasamɛntɔ
no casamento,
for my wedding,

jɛj pɔz miɾa maɾika
y hei...Pos mira, Marica,
and I will...then look, Marica,

βaj pɔr un nɛtɔ
vai por un neto,
go for a glass of wine,

ɛantɾamɛntaz nɔn kitas
e antramentas non quitas
and as long as not you abandon
(and as long as you don't give up)

ɛsɛs θɛɾɛʎɔs
eses cerellos,
these ideas,

jas pitaz βam mɛðɾandɔ
y as pitas van medrando
and chickens are growing up

kɔ ɣalɔ nɛɣɾɔ
c'ó galo negro,
with the cock black,
(with the black cock,)

paɾa pɔɲɛlɔs ɔβɔs
para poñel-os hovos,
to lay their eggs,

ɛ tɔðɔ akɛlɔ
e todo aquelo
and all that

dɔ ʃanɛjɾɔ ðɔs kartɔs
d'ò Xaneiro, d'os cartos,
about January, about the money,

jɔ kasamɛntɔ
y ò casamento,
and about the wedding,

miɲa pɾɛnda da alma
miña prenda da alma,
love of my life,

bamɔz βeβɛndɔ
¡vamos bebendo!
let's go drinking!

Idiomatic translation:
I have three white hens and a black cock. In time, they will lay many eggs, and I will sell them at a good price in January and I will get enough money for a long veil, and I will wear it for my wedding and I will...look Marica, go for a glass of wine, and as long as one doesn't give up, and the chickens are growing up with the black cock to lay their eggs, and all that I said about January, about the money, and about the wedding, love of my life, let's go drinking!

Notes

1. Cecilia Rodrigo, E-mail to author, October 5, 1998.
2. Philip Ward, ed., The Oxford *Companion to Spanish Literature*. (Oxford: Clarendon Press, 1978), 110.
3. Federico Jimenez Losantos, "Rosalia de Castro," *Cronica*, Sunday, October 4, 1998, *El Mundo* (section), trans. by author, 24.

Chapter 16

Triptico de Mosén Cinto

tríptikɔ ðə mɔsən θintɔ

Triptico de Mosén Cinto (1946)	10:20
Triptych from Mosén Cinto	
L'harpa sagrada	3:50
Lo violí de Sant Francesch	2:50
Sant Francesc i la cigala	3:40

Vocal Range: B^3 to G^5
For voice and orchestra or voice and piano

Orchestra: 2 flutes (2nd doubling piccolo), 1 oboe, 1 English horn, 1 B-flat clarinet, 1 bassoon, 2 horns in F, 2 trumpets in C, snare drum, harp, celesta,violins I and II, violas, violoncellos, double basses.

Triptico de Mosén Cinto was premiered in the Palace of Music in Barcelona in October 1946, by the famous soprano Victoria de los Angeles. The Rodrigos had heard her in concert when she was only twenty years old and had marveled at her sense of style and sensitivity.[1] The Municipal Orchestra of Barcelona was conducted by Eduardo Toldrá.[2]

    Jacinto Verdaguer (1845-1902), born in Folgueroles, Barcelona, was a major Catalan poet of the time. His poetry established Catalan as a modern literary language, capable of depth of expression and nuance. His two great epic poems, *Atlàntida*, which won first prize at the Jocs Florals in 1877, and his *Canigó*, in 1885, were popular nationalist works.[3]

lərpə saɣraðа

1. L'harpa sagrada
The Sacred Harp

ə lərβɾə ðiβi
A L'Arbre diví
From the tree divine
(From the divine tree)

pənzəðə nes lərpə
Penjada n'és l'Harpa.
Hung thus is the harp.
(thus is hung the harp.)

lərpə ðə ðəβid
L'Harpa de David,
The harp of David,

ən siun əmaðə
En Sion amada.
In Zion beloved.
(In beloved Zion.)

son kləβjər ez ðɔr
Son clavier és d'or,
Its clavier (frame) is of gold,

səs kurðəz ðə plate
Ses cordes de plata,
Its strings of silver,

məs kɔm alɣun təmps
Mes, com algun temps,
But, for some time,

ʒə ləmɔr nɔ i kəntə
Ja l'amor no hi canta,
The love not here sing,
(It has not sung of love,)

kə i fə sɛt ʒəmɛks
Que hi fa set gemecs
Here it makes a groaning
(It sings a lament)

də ðɔl i əɲuransə
De dol i enyorança.
Of grief and ignorance.

suβrin lus sɛl
S'obrien los cels,
Opens the heavens,
(The heavens open,)

limfɛrn sə təŋkaβə
L'infern se tancava,
Hell closes,

jəl kɔr ðə sɔn deu
I al cor de son Déu
And to the heart of his God
(and to God's heart)

lə tɛrra es ʎiɣəðə
La terra és lligada.
The earth is bound.

ə lultimə ʒəmɛk
A l'últim gemec
At the last groan

lu ðiə səpəɣə
Lo dia s'apaga,
The day is extinguished,

jəs trəŋkən luz rɔks
I es trenquen los rocs
And it breaks the stones

tupənt lun əm ləltɾə
Topant l'un amb l'altre.
Falling the one with the other.
(Falling one over another.)

təmbes trəŋkə əl kɔr
També es trenca el cor
Also it breaks the heart

duna bɛrʒə maɾə
D'una Verge Mare
Of the Virgin Mary

kəskultənt lus suns
Que, escoltant los sons,
Who, listening to the sounds,

ə lombrə plurəβə
A l'ombra plorava:
In the shade weeping: (She says:)
(weeps in the shade:)

anʒələtz ðəl səl
Angelets del cel,
Little angels of the heavens,

dəspənʒawmə lərpə
Despenjau-me L'Harpa,
Unhook to me the harp,
(Unhook the harp for me,)

kə ðə tan əmun
Que de tan amunt
That of so high
(because it is so high)

no puk əβasta lə
No puc abastar-la;
Not I am able to reach;
(I am not able to reach it;)

bəʃau lə si us plaw
Baixau-la, si us plau,
Lower it, if you please,

məz ðə βɾaŋkə ən βɾaŋkə
Mes de branca en branca,
But from branch to branch,

no səsfluɾən pas
No s'esfloren pas
Not they break
(they do not break)

səs kurðəz ni kaʃə
Ses cordes ni caixa.
Its strings nor its frame.

puzaw la ən mon pit
Posau-la en mon pit,
Put it on my breast,

kə puɣə tuka lə
Que puga tocar-la;
That I may play it;

si ə pɛɾðut lu sɔ
Si ha perdut lo so,
If has lost its sound,
(If it has lost its sound,)

li turnəre ən karə
Li tornaré encara;
I will return it again;

si no lə pɛrðut
Si no l'ha perdut,
If not it has lost,
(If it has not lost it,)

murire əβrəsant lə
Moriré abraçant-la
I will die embracing it

lə meβə ərpə dɔr
Le meva Harpa d'or
The harp of gold

kəl mɔn ələɣrabə
Que el món alegrava!
Let the world be happy!

Idiomatic translation:
The divine harp of David hangs from a tree in Zion. Although it is
made of gold with silver strings, it has not played a love song for a
long time. Instead, it plays a mournful lament. As it plays, the
heavens open, the door to hell closes, and earth is bound to God's
spirit. With the final note, the day ends and even the stones break
with sadness. The Virgin Mary listens and pleads with the angels to
gently hand her the harp. If the harp is unplayable, she will return it.
If it has not lost its sound, the Virgin will place it on her breast and
will die embracing it, bringing happiness to the world.

lu biuli də santə frənsɛsk
II. **Lo violí de Sant Francesc**
The Violin of Saint Francis of Assisi

də grɛsiə ən lu pəseβrə
De Grecio en lo pessebre,
Of Greece at the manger
(At the manger in Greece)

dəβan lumfan diβi
davant l'Infant diví,
in front of the Infant divine,
(before the divine Infant,)

roŋkə lə kurnəmuzə
Ronca la cornamusa,
Hoarse the bagpipe,

sunə lu təmbori
Sona lo tamborí,
Sound the tambourine,

lə flawtə jəspiɣeʒə
La flauta hi espigueja,
The flute springs up like ears of corn,

lə flawtəj lu flawti
La flauta i lo flautí.
The flute and the piccolos.

lə pəsturel lə ðulsə
La pastorel, la dolca
The shepherdess, the sweet

frənsɛsk lə bɔl səɣi
Francesc la vol seguir.
Frances the flight pursues.
(St. Francis follows the shepherdess.)

no re fərɛtz ni graʎə
No té ferrets ni gralla,
Not he has triangle nor clarinet,
(He has neither triangle nor clarinet,)

geʎa ni βənduli
Gralla ni bandolí.
Clarinet nor mandolin.

kul dɔz βəstons truβə
Cull dos bastons que troba
He picks up two sticks that he finds

ʎənsatz bɔrəl kəmi
Llençats vora el camí,
Throw at the edge the path,
(Thrown at the edge of the path,)

sən puzə un ə ləspaʎʎə
Se'n posa un a l'espatlla
He puts one on his shoulder

ə taʎ də biuli
A tall de violí,
to cut the violin,
(Like a violin,)

pəsən ləltrə pər soβrə
Passant l'altre per sobre
Passes the other by over
(Passing the other over it)

kɔm un dɔr fi
com un arquet d'or fi.
like a bow of gold fine.

lu biuli ez ðə freʃə
Lo violí és de freixe,
The violin is of ash,

lərkɛt dun brot ðə pi
L'arquet d'un brot de pi,
The bow of a shoot of pine,

məs ən səz mans səɣradəs
Mes en ses mans sagrades
But in his hands holy
(But in his holy hands)

gran muzikə surti
Gran música en sortí.
Great music emerges.

no nə ðəʃi ðə muzikə
¿No n'ha d'eixir de música,
Hasn't the emergence of music,
(Doesn't music emerge,)

si əls tukə un sərəfi
Si els toca un Serafí?
If it plays a seraph?
(if a Seraph plays it?)

Idiomatic translation:
   At the manger in Greece, many instruments play--the bagpipe, the
tambourine, the flute, and piccolos. St. Francis of Assisi follows the
sweet shepherdess to the manger. There is no triangle, clarinet, or
mandolin. The Saint picks up two sticks and holds them like a
violin, pretending to play. The sticks are only ash, but in his holy
hands, great music emerges. Can't an angel make wonderful music?

sant fransɛsk i lə siɣalə
III. Sant Francesc i la cigala
St. Francis and the Cicada

lu kumben es tan pətit
Lo convent és tan petit
The convent is so little

kə unə sərmənt əŋgərlandə
Que una serment l'engarlanda,
that a single vine it adorns,
(that a single vine adorns it,)

ɔn un diəl pik ðəl sɔl
On un dia al pic del sol
Where one day at the peak of the sun

sɔw kəntə unə siɣalə
S'ou cantar una cigala.
It is heard singing a cicada.
(A cicada is heard singing.)

ziɣəluzət
Zigaluzet.
Little shepherd.

ʒə li kriðə sant fransɛsk
Ja li crida Sant Francesc:
Already to her calls St. Francis:
(St. Francis calls to her:)

binə binə ɔ mə ʒərmana
Vine, vine, oh ma germana;
Come, come, oh my sister;

binə i kəntə unə kənsɔ
Vine i canta una cançó
come and sing a song

əl βɔn deu kə tə kriaðа
Al bon Déu que t'ha criada.
To the good God that to you raised.
(To the good Lord who has raised you.)

ziɣəluzət
Zigaluzet.
Little shepherd.

lə siɣalə no fəl sɔrt
La cigala no fa el sort,
The cicada does not go out,
(The cicada does not run away,)

soβɾə sus dits sə puzabə
Sobre sos dits se posava,
On her toes she stood

i kantə kə kəntəras
I canta que cantarás
She was not stopping singing
(And she sang and sang)

lə kənsɔ ðə ləstiwaðə
La cançó de l'estiuada.
The song of summer.

ziɣəluzət
Zigaluzet.
Little shepherd.

kaðə ðiə əl dəməti
Cada dia al dematí
Every day at morning

βrunziðɔrə rəðəbaʎə
Brunzidora redevalla;
She went back down buzzing

kwan bujt ði əs sɔn pəsats
Quan vuit di es són passats
When eight days are passed

ʒe li ðiw tɔt əmuʃanʎə
Ja li diu tot amoixanlla:
He to her says, caressing her:
(He says to her, caressing her:)

ziɣəluzət
Zigaluzet.
Little shepherd.

siɣalo bɔn siɣalɑ
"Cigaló, bon cigaló,
Big cicada, good big cicada,

təm səntit unə buitaðə
T'hem sentit una vuitada;
you we have heard eight days;
(we have heard you for eight days;)

ɔn deu tə buʎə arə bes
On Deu te vulla ara ves
Where God you wants now to go
(Go where God wants you to go)

ə puntəʒa lə ɣitarrə
A puntejar la guitarra.
To pluck the guitar.

ziɣəluzət
Zigaluzet.
Little shepherd.

Idiomatic translation:
    The convent is so small that a single vine can encircle it. A cicada
sang one day when the sun was at its peak. Little shepherd. St.
Francis called to the cicada, "Come, oh come, my sister and sing a

song to the good Lord who raised you." Little shepherd. The cicada did not run away but stood on tiptoe and sang the song of summer. Little shepherd. Every morning, she awakened and at the end of a week, the shepherd said, "Good cicada, you stayed a week. Now go where God wants you. You may now play the guitar as well as sing."

Notes

1. Victoria Kamhi, *Hand in Hand with Joaquin Rodrigo, My Life at the Maestro's Side,* trans. Ellen Wilkerson (Pittsburgh: Latin American Literary Review Press, 1992), 130.

2. Kamhi, *Hand in Hand,* 134-135.

3. Philip Ward, ed., The Oxford *Companion to Spanish Literature.* (Oxford: Clarendon Press, 1978), 604.

Chapter 17

Villancicos

bi ʎanθikɔs

Villancicos	5:10
Christmas Carols	
Pastorcito Santo	2:00
Aire y donaire	1:40
Coplillas de Belén	1:30

Vocal Range: D$^{\#4}$ to F$^{\#5}$

For voice with piano accompaniment or guitar accompaniment

Maestro Rodrigo is particularly fond of "Pastorcito Santo" and considers this his best song, after "Cantico de la esposa."[1] Victoria de los Angeles especially liked "Pastorcito Santo" and "Coplillas de Belén" and included these *villancicos* in many of her concerts. Victoria Kamhi writes:

> On the tenth of January, 1957, we went to a concert of the National Orchestra, conducted by Argenta, in which Victoria de los Angeles, at the peak of her career, was brilliant.
> Our daughter, at the time an avid autograph collector, insisted on getting one from the hands of the illustrious singer, and Joaquín had no choice but to call the hotel where she was staying. He spoke with her husband, Enrique Magriñá, to ask this

favor, and told him as well, that he had composed two songs that she had not yet heard.

"If that is so" replied Enrique, "we will come to your house right now and pick them up."

The pleasant visit lasted more than two hours, as we chatted and listened to Joaquín's records. Victoria told us that she was going to sing in Paris on February 2nd, and that she would put "Pastorcito Santo" and "Coplillas de Belén" on her program. Beginning on that date, she sang them in all her concerts, and thanks to her unique art, they toured the world.[2]

"Pastorcito Santo," Lope de Vega, poet, is dedicated to Jack Schermant, the Rodrigo family dentist and a great music lover.

"Aire y donaire" is the most difficult of the three songs with its ostinato accompaniment. It is a setting of anonymous poetry adapted by Victoria Kamhi and is dedicated to Maria Morales, the soprano who sang the premier of "¿De dónde venís, amore?"

"Coplillas de Belén," Victoria Kamhi, poet, is dedicated to Juan Harguindey in the Rodrigo edition. Juan Harguindey was Victoria Kamhi's obstetrician, and he saved Ms. Kamhi's life and the life of her unborn child, Cecilia. When Victoria Kamhi developed phlebitis during the seventh month of pregnancy, Juan Harguindey prescribed bed rest and ordered her to wear a brace on her afflicted leg. The condition was especially frightening because just a few months earlier, Victoria Kamhi had given birth to a stillborn daughter. The Rodrigos are especially grateful to Juan Harguindey.[3]

In the Schott edition, this song is dedicated to Gloria Franco Alonso, the wife of the orchestra conductor Odón Alonso, who premiered the *Villancicos* in their orchestral version.

As stated in Chapter Three, entitled "Canciones," "La Espera" is often performed with *Villancicos* in this order, "La Espera," "Aire y donaire," "Coplillas de Belén," and "Pastorcito Santo." The set is then called *Cuatro Villancicos*.[4]

pastɔrθitɔ santɔ
I. **Pastorcito Santo**
Holy Shepherd Boy

θaɣalɛxɔ ðɛ pɛrlas
Zagalejo de perlas,
Young lad of pearls,

ixɔ ðɛl alβa
hijo del alba
son of dawn

dɔndɛ βajs kɛ aθɛ fɾiɔ
¿dónde vais que hace frío
where do you go that it is cold

tan dɛ maɲana
tan de mañana?
so early this morning?

kɔmɔ sɔjs luθɛɾɔ
Como sois lucero
As you are the light

ðɛl alβa mia
del alba mía,
of dawn my,
(of my dawn,)

a tɾaɛr ɛl dia
a traer el día
to bring the day

naθɛjs pɾimɛɾɔ
naceis primero;
you are born first;

pastɔr j kɔrðɛɾɔ
pastor y cordero,
shepherd and lamb,

sin tʃɔθa ni lana
sin choza ni lana,
without hovel or wool,
(a choza is a hut made of tiered straw in a conical shape)

dɔndɛ βajs kɛ aθɛ fɾiɔ
¿dónde vais que hace frío,
where do you go that it is cold,

tan dɛ maɲana
tan de mañana?
so early this morning?

pɛrlas ɛn lɔs ɔxɔs
Perlas en los ojos,
Pearls in the eyes,

risa ɛn la βɔka
risa en la boca,
laughter on the mouth,

a plaθɛr jɛnɔxɔz
a placer y enojos
to pleasure and annoyance

las almas prɔβɔka
las almas provoca;
the souls provoke;

kaβeʎitɔz rɔxɔs
cabellitos rojos,
little hair red,
(little red hair,)

bɔka ðɛ ɣɾana
boca de grana
mouth of scarlet

dɔndɛ βajs kɛ aθɛ fɾiɔ
¿dónde vais que hace frío,
where do you go that it is cold,

tan dɛ maɲana
tan de mañana?
so early this morning?

kɛ tɛnɛjs kɛ aθɛr
¿Que tenéis que hacer,
What do you have to do,

pastɔrθitɔ santɔ
¡pastorcito santo!
holy shepherd boy!

maðɾuyandɔ tantɔ
madrugando tanto?
getting up so early?

lɔ ðais a ɛntɛndɛr
Lo dais a entender,
You give it to be understood,

auŋkɛ βajs a βɛr
aunque váis a ver
although you will see

ðisfɾaθaðɔ al alma
disfrazado al alma.
disguised to the soul.

dɔndɛ βajs kɛ aθɛ fɾiɔ
¿Dónde vais que hace frío,
Where do you go that it is cold,

tan dɛ maɲana
tan de mañana?
so early this morning?

Idiomatic translation:
   Little shepherd boy, son of dawn, where are you going so early on this cold morning? You bring the dawn and light to earth with your birth, shepherd and lamb without a coat or hut. Where are you going so early on this cold morning?
   With pearls in your eyes and a laughing mouth, with red hair and scarlet lips, you provoke souls to pleasure and annoyance. Where are you going so early on this cold morning?
   What causes you to get up early, holy shepherd boy? You expect us to understand, although you will see the soul disguised. Where are you going so early on this cold morning?

ajɾɛ i ðɔnajɾɛ

II. Aire y donaire
Airs and Graces

ajɾɛj ðɔnajɾɛ
Aire y donaire,
Airs and graces,

xitaniʎas al βajlɛ al βajlɛ
gitanillas, al baile, al baile,
Little gypsies, dance, dance,

ajɾɛj ðɔnajɾɛ tɔkaj rɛpika
aire y donaire toca y repica,
airs and graces play and ring,

sɔnaxwɛlas i kastaɲɛtikas
sonajuelas y castañeticas.
timbrels and castanets.

aj kɛ tamaɲɔ
¡Ay, qué tamaño!
Ay, how big!

nɔ lɛ ʎɛɣa xwanikɔ al θapatɔ
No le llega Juanico al zapato.
No he arrives little Juan to the shoe.
(Little Juan isn't as big as the shoe.)

aj kɛ tamaɲɔ
¡Ay, qué tamaño!
Ay, how big!

aj kɛ θaɣala
¡Ay, qué zagala,
Ay, what shepherdess,

kwantɔ βa kɛs su maðɾɛ sin falta
cuanto vá que es su madre sin falta!
it must be that is his mother without doubt!

andɛ kɔrra siɣa
Ande, corra, siga
Go, run, follow

sɔnaxwɛlas i kastaɲɛtikas
sonajuelas y castañeticas
timbrels and castanets

xitaniʎas al βajlɛ
gitanillas al baile,
little gypsies dance,

ajɾɛj ðɔnajɾɛ
aire y donaire.
airs and graces.

aj kɛ βwɛn βjɛxɔ
¡Ay, qué buen viejo!
Ay, what a good old man!

kɛ a tɛniðɔ sus flɔɾɛs ɛs θjɛrtɔ
Que ha tenido sus flores es cierto.
that he has had his flowers, it is certain.

aj kɛ animalɛs
¡Ay! qué animales
Ay, what animals

kɔmɔ a kɛstɔs aj mil sɛmɛxantɛs
como aquestos hay mil semejantes!
why there are thousands to me!

ajɾɛj ðɔnajɾɛ
¡Aire y donaire,
Airs and grace,

tɔkaj rɛpika
toca y repica,
play and sing,

sɔnaxwɛlas i kastaɲɛtikas
sonajuelas y castañeticas,
timbrels and castanets,

xitaniʎas al βajlɛ al βajlɛ
gitanillas al baile, al baile!
little gypsies dance, dance!

ajɛj ðɔnajɾɛ
¡Aire y donaire!
Airs and graces!

Idiomatic translation:
Airs and graces! Little gypsies dance and play your timbrels and castanets. Oh, how big, little Juan hardly reaches his sandal. Oh, the shepherdess must be his mother. Airs and graces, play and ring your timbrels and castanets, little gypsies. Dance! Go, run, follow the dance and play your timbrels and castanets, little gypsies, with airs and graces.
Oh, what a good old man! He must have been handsome in his youth. Airs and graces! Oh, what animals. There must be thousands of them. Airs and graces, play and ring your castanets, little gypsies. Dance! Airs and graces!

kɔpliʎaz ðɛ βɛlɛn
III. Coplillas de Belén
Carols of Bethlehem

si la palmɛɾa supjɛɾa
Si la palmera supiera
If the palm tree knew

kɛ al niɲɔ ɛŋ kuna tam bɛʎa
que al Niño en cuna tan bella
that the Boy in the cradle so pretty

kaiðɔ sɛ lɛa una ɛstɾɛʎa
caído se le ha una estrella,
falls itself has a star,
(a star falls for him,)

su aβaniko lɛ tɛndjɛɾa
su abanico le tendiera
its fan to him tends
(its fan tends him)

paɾa kɛl niɲɔ mɛθjɛɾa
para que el Niño meciera.
so that the Boy shall sway.

dɛl mɔntɛ pɔr la laðɛɾa
Del monte por la ladera,
Of the mountain by the slope,

kɛ alɛɣɾɛ βa ɛl pastɔrθiʎɔ
qué alegre va el pastorcillo,
how cheerfully goes the shepherd boy,

mɔntaðɔ ɛn su βɔrrikiʎɔ
montado en su borriquillo.
riding on his little donkey.

kɔrrɛ kɛl niɲɔ tɛspɛra
¡Corre, que el Niño te espera
Run, the Boy waits for you

jɛs kɔrta la nɔtʃɛ βwɛna
y es corta la Noche buena!
and it is short Christmas Eve!
(and Christmas Eve is short!)

ɛm bɛlɛn la βirxɛn puɾa
En Belén la Virgen pura
In Bethlehem the Virgin pure

la rɛθal niɲɔ kɛspɛɾa
le reza al Niño que espera.
prays to the Boy that waits.

kanta la βirxɛn maɾia
Canta la Virgen María
Sings the Virgin Mary

εl niɲɔ lɛ sɔnrɛia
el Niño le sonreía,
and the Boy smiles,

kɛ tɾistɛsta la palmɛɾa
Qué triste está la palmera.
How sad is the palm tree.

si la palmɛɾa supjɛɾa
Si la palmera supiera
If the palm tree knew

lɔ kɛspɛɾa
lo que espera...
it that waits...
(what awaits it...)

Idiomatic translation:
If the palm tree knew that the pretty Boy in the cradle was a star from heaven, it would fan him with its leaves, lulling him to sleep.
The happy shepherd boy rides on his little donkey down the mountain. Run, shepherd boy, for the Infant is waiting for you and Christmas Eve is short!
In Bethlehem, the Virgin Mary prays to the Boy. She sings and the Boy smiles. The palm tree would be so sad if it only knew that for which it waits.

Notes

1. Cecilia Rodrigo, E-mail to author, April 23, 1998.
2. Victoria Kamhi, *Hand in Hand with Joaquín Rodrigo, My Life at the Maestro's Side*, trans. Ellen Wilkerson (Pittsburgh: Latin American Literary Review Press, 1992), 166.
3. Kamhi, *Hand in Hand*, 112.
4. Cecilia Rodrigo, interview with author, July 26, 1998.

Selected Discography

Complete Songs, The (Vol. 1)
Con Antonio Machado, Doce canciones españolas, Dos canciones para cantar a los niños, Dos villancicos, La espera. Margarita Castor-Alberty/Carlos Cebro. LYS.
Canción del grumete, Cántico de la esposa, Cuatro canciones populares españolas, Cuatro madrigales amatorios, Esta niña se lleva la flor, Villancicos. Patricia Rozario/Mark Troop. Collins Classics 30522.
Canción del grumete, Cántico de la esposa, Cuatro madrigales amatorios, Esta niña se lleva la flor, Estribillo, Fino cristal, Serranilla, Sobre el cupey, Tres villancicos. Ana Higueras, Miguel Zanetti. Tempo.
Canciones del Marqués
En Aranjuez con tu amor, Pastorcito santo, Coplillas de Belén, Aire y donaire, En Jerez de la Frontera, Adela, De ronda, Romance de Durandarte, Folías Canarias, Coplas del pastor enamorado. Lucienn van Deyck/Wim Brioen. Vanguard Classics.
Coplillas de Belén, Pastorcito santo, Adela, Coplas del pastor enamorado. Manuel Barrueco/Philharmonia Orchestra/Plácido Domingo. EMI Classics.
Coplillas de Belén, Pastorcito santo, Tres canciones españolas, I. Garcisanz, a. Ponce, guitar. Arion 68197.
Cuatro canciones sefardíes. Victoria de los Angeles, Geoffrey

Parsons. CBS masterworks S 76833.

Cuatro madrigales amatorios. Victoria de los Angeles/Orchestre de la Société des Concerts du Conservatorie/Rafael Frübeck de Burgos. EMI.

___. Montserrat Caballé, Miguel Zanetti, Alhambra.

Doce canciones populares. Marimí Pozo, Victoria Kamhi, and Joaquín Rodrigo. Columbia.

Domingo, Placido. *En Aranjuez con tu amor*. Polystar.

___. *The Best of José Carreras*, Erato 21667.

___. *Montserrat Caballé*, RCA Victor Red Seal 61044.

Dos poemas. Yolanda Marcolescou, Robert Goodberg, Orion.

Tríptic de Mosén Cinto
Victoria de los Angeles/Orchestre des Concerts Lamoreux/Rafael Frübeck de Burgos. EMI.

Video

"Shadows and Light:" Joaquín Rodrigo at 90/Concierto de Aranjuez. Rhombus Media, Inc. (1993) Phillips.

Bibliography

Amo, Joaquín Arnau, Ramon Barce, Enrique Bátiz, Raymond Calcraft, Antonio Fernández-Cid, Enrique Franco, Antonio Iglesias, Claudio Prieto, Ariel Ramírez, Pepe Romero, Albert Sardá, and Alberto González Lapuente. *Joaquín Rodrigo: A Compilation of Articles for the 90th Anniversary.* Translated by Elizabeth Matthews and Raymond Calcraft. Madrid, Spain: Sociedad General de Autores de España, 1992.

Binkley, Thomas, and Margit Frenk. *Spanish Romances of the Sixteenth Century.* Bloomington: Indiana University Press, 1995.

Brenan, Gerald. *The Literature of the Spanish People.* Cambridge, Mass.: Cambridge University Press, 1953.

Bunce, Tina Sandor. "Joaquin Rodrigo's Cuatro Madrigales Amatorios." Bowling Green State University, dissertation, 1985.

Butterfield, Jeremy, Mike Gonzalez, Gerry Breslin, Teresa Alvarez Garcia, Brian Steel, Ana Cristina Llompart, and José Miguel Galván Déniz. *Harper Collins Spanish Concise Dictionary.* Glasgow, Scotland: HarperCollins Publishers, 1998.

Calderon, Fina de. *Fuego, Grito, Luna: Federico Garcia Lorca: poema en tres letras/de Fina de Calderon.* Malaga, Spain: Ediciones Litoral, 1977.

Carman, Judith. "Music Reviews." *Journal of Singing* 53:5 (May/June 1997): 59-62.

Castel, Nico. *A Singer's Manual of Spanish Lyric Diction.* New

York: Excalibur Publishing, 1994.

Chandler, Richard E., and Kessel Schwartz. *A New History of Spanish Literature*, revised edition. Baton Rouge: Louisiana State University Press, 1991.

Chase, Gilbert. *Spanish Music*. New York: Dover, 1959.

Cockburn, Jacqueline, and Richard Stokes. *The Spanish Song Companion*. London: Victor Gollancz Ltd., 1992.

Cohen, J. M. *The Penguin Book of Spanish Verse*. Bucks: Penguin, 1988.

Collins Spanish-English Dictionary. Edited by Colin Smith. London: 1971.

Cox, Richard G. *The Singer's Manual of German and French Diction*. New York: G. Schirmer, 1970.

Dozy, Reinhart. *Spanish Islam: A History of the Moslems in Spain*, translated by Frances Griffin Stokes. New York: Duffield, 1913.

Draayer, Suzanne R. Collier. "Contemporary Spanish Song: Cycles for Soprano by Joaquín Turina and Joaquín Rodrigo." D.M.A. dissertation, University of Maryland, College Park, 1987.

___."Joaquín Rodrigo and his *Doce Canciones Españolas* and *Cantos de amor y de guerra.*" *The NATS Journal* 51:4 (March/April 1995): 5-17.

Emié, Louis. *Dialogues avec Max Jacob*. Christine van Rogger Andreucci, postface. Bordeaux, France: Le Festin, 1994.

___. *Espagnes: Essais/Louis Emié*. Avant-propos de Bernard Delvaille. Castelnau-le-Lez, France: Climats, 1991.

Fox, Dian. *Refiguring the Hero*. University Park: Pennsylvania State University Press, 1991.

Grubb,Thomas. *Singing in French*. New York: Schirmer Books, 1979.

Hispanic Literature Criticism, vol.1. Edited by Jelena Krstovíc, Detroit, Mich.: Gale Research Inc., 1994.

Kamhi, Victoria. *Hand in Hand with Joaquin Rodrigo, My Life at the Maestro's Side*, translated by Ellen Wilkerson. Pittsburgh, Pa.: Latin American Literary Review Press, 1992.

Losantos, Federico Jimenez. "Rosalia de Castro." *Cronica*, Sunday, October 4, 1998, *El Mundo* (section) translation by author, 24.

Machado, Antonio. *Selected Poems*, translated by Alan S. Trueblood. Cambridge: Harvard University Press, 1982.

March, Ivan. "Beyond Aranjuez: Joaquín Rodrigo talks to Ivan March." *Gramophone* 40 (July 1992): 10-11.

Marco, Tomás. "Joaquín Rodrigo." *The New Grove's Dictionary of Music and Musicians*, 6th ed. 20 vols., ed. Stanley Sadie. London: Macmillan, 1980.

McGee, Timothy, ed., with A. G. Rigg and David N. Klausner. *Singing Early Music---the Pronunciation of European Languages in the Late Middle Ages and Renaissance*. Bloomington: Indiana University Press, 1996

Newcomb, Larry. "Joaquín Rodrigo and Spanish Nationalism." University of Florida, dissertation, 1995. 114pp.

Powell, Linton E. *A History of Spanish Piano Music.* Bloomington: Indiana University Press, 1980.

Rodrigo, Cecilia. E-mails to author, March 1998-January 1999.

___.Interviews with author, July 1998.

Rodrigo, Joaquín. *Aranjuez, ma pensée,* Madrid: Ediciones Joaquín Rodrigo. 1988.

___. *En Aranjuez con tu amor.* Madrid: Union Musical Ediciones, S.L. 1971.

___. *Barcarola.* Mainz: Schott. 1995.

___. *Cáncion del cucu.* Mainz: Schott. 1995.

___. *Cáncion del grumete.* Mainz: Schott. 1995.

___. *Canciones de dos épocas.* Mainz: Schott. 1928 renewed 1955.

___. *Cántico de la esposa.* Mainz: Schott. 1995.

___. *Cantos de amor y de guerra.* Madrid: Union Musical Ediciones, S.L. 1969.

___. *La Chanson de ma vie.* Madrid: Ediciones Joaquín Rodrigo. 1939.

___. *Chimères.* Paris: Editions Max Eschig. 1939.

___. *Con Antonio Machado.* Madrid: Union Musical Ediciones, S.L. 1986.

___. *Coplas del pastor enamorado.* Mainz: Schott. 1995.

___. *Cuatre cançons en llengua catalana.* Mainz: Schott. 1989.

___. *Cuatro madrigales amatorios.* London: J&W Chester. 1960.

___. *Cuatro canciones sefardíes.* Madrid: Ediciones Joaquín Rodrigo. 1992.

___. *Doce canciones españolas.* Mainz: Schott. 1995.

___. *Dos canciones para cantar a los niños.* Madrid: Union Musical Ediciones, S.L. 1980.

___. *Dos Poemas.* Madrid: Union Musical Ediciones, S.L. 1992.

___. *La espera.* Mainz: Schott. 1972.

___. *Esta Niña se lleva la flor.* Mainz: Schott. 1995.

___. *Estribillo.* Mainz: Schott. 1993.

___. *Fino cristal.* Mainz: Schott. 1995.

___. *Folias Canarias.* Mainz: Schott. 1959.

___. *La grotte.* Boca Raton: Masters Music Publications, Inc. 1991.

___. *Líricas castellanas.* Mainz: Schott. 1995.

___. *Por mayo, era por mayo (Romancillo).* Madrid: Ediciones Joaquín Rodrigo. 1960.

___. *Primavera*. Madrid: Ediciones Joaquín Rodrigo. 1995.

___. *Romance de Comendador de Ocana*. Madrid: Union Musical Ediciones, S.L. 1962.

___. *Romance de Durandarte*. Madrid: Ediciones Joaquín Rodrigo. 1995.

___. *Rosaliana*. Mainz: Schott. 1990.

___. *Sobre el cupey*. Mainz: Schott. 1995.

___. *Soneto*. Mainz: Schott. 1995.

___. *Tres villancicos*. Mainz: Schott. 1995.

___. *Triptico de Mosén Cinto*. Mainz: Schott. 1996.

___. ¡*Un Home, San Antonio!* Mainz: Schott. 1995.

Romero, Justo. "Joaquín Rodrigo, El Hombre y el Músico." *Monsalvat* 175 (October 1989): 12-13.

Salem, Richard. "Blind Pianist Rodrigo Plays His Own Music." *Washington Post and Times Herald*. April 13, 1958, A(7).

Sobrer, Josep Miquel, and Edmon Colomer. *The Singers' Anthology of Twentieth Century Spanish Song*. New York: Helion Press, 1987.

Sopeña, Federico. *Joaquín Rodrigo*. Madrid: Dirección General de Bellas Artes, 1970.

___. *Joaquín Rodrigo*. Madrid: Ediciones y Publicaciones Españolas, S.A. 1946.

Starkie, Walter. *Spain: A Musician's Journey through Time and Space*, 2 vols. Geneva, Switzerland: Edisli, 1958.

Tello, Francisco Jose Leon. "La Estetica de la Musica Vocal de Joaquín Rodrigo: Catorce Canciones para canto y Piano." *Cuadernos Hispanoamericanos* N355, 1980, 70-106.

Ticknor, George. *History of Spanish Literature*, 6th ed. 3 vols. New York: Gordian Press, Inc., 1965.

Times (London), "A Modern Spanish Composer." May 19, 1958, C(14).

Vega, Lope de. *Five Plays*. Translated by Jill Booty. New York: Hill and Wang, 1961.

Vilanova, Núria, Núria Font, Raphael Davies, Teresa Udina, and Anna Jené. *Compact Dictionary English-Catalan*. Barcelona, Spain: Vox, 1997.

Wall, Joan, Robert Caldwell, Tracy Gavilanes, and Sheila Allen. *Diction for Singers*. Dallas, Tex.: Pst...Inc., 1990.

Ward, Philip, ed. The Oxford *Companion to Spanish Literature*. Oxford, England: Clarendon Press, 1978.

General Index

Albéniz, Isaac 3
Alemán, Fedora 158, 195, 205
Alonso, Gloria Franco 244
Alonso, Odón 111, 244
Andujar, Carmen 145
D'Andurain, Pedro 19
Angeles, Victoria de los 7, 80, 82, 231, 243-244
Antich, Francisco 2
Aquino, Luis Hernandez 80
Aragón, Lola Rodriguez 18, 71, 166
Asencio, Vicente 111
Attar, Josefina (Fina de Calderón) 106
Ausencias de dulcinea 5, 7
Azucena de quito, La 6

Badia, Conchita 19, 60
Benardete, M. J. 158
Berg, Alban 19
Berganza, Teresa 7, 166, 195

Caballé, Montserrat 7
Calderón, Fina de 91, 106

Camp, Juan 40
Cancioneros 172
Capriccio 5
Carner, Josep 35-36, 146
Castro, Rosalía de 85, 217-218
Chávarri, Eduardo López 2, 145
Cid, Antonio Fernández 84
Cid, María 17
Cinco piezas infantiles 2, 15
Cinco sonatas de Castilla con tocatta a modo de pregón 6
Collet, Henri 2
Columbus, Christopher 34
Concierto de Aranjuez 5, 17, 23 26
Concierto de Estio 5
Concierto en modo galante 6
Concierto heroico 5
Concierto serenata 6, 19
Cruz, San Juan de la 37
Cuatro danzas de españa 16
Cuatro piezas para piano 17

Debussy, Claude 205
Diego, Gerardo 36, 146

D'Indy, Vincent 14
"Dos canciones sefardíes del
    siglo XV" 157
Dukas, Paul 2, 6, 16
Durias, Cármen Pérez 166

El Hijo fingido 6, 19
Emié, Louis 205
Falla, Manual de 3, 4, 6
Fantasia para un gentilhombre
    6, 19
Figueroa, Francisco de 54
Foix, Germana de 69

Galindo, Blas 19
Granados, Enrique 4
Gran Marcha de los
    subsecretarios 18
Grieg, Edvard 18
Guasch, Joan 146

Halffter, Ernesto 5
Harguindey, Juan 18, 244
Heguey, Geza 14
Higueras, Ana 111, 211, 217
Homenaje a la tempranica 18

Jiménez, Juan Ramón 195-196
Jorda, Enrique 19
Juglares 2

Kamhi, Isaac 158
Kamhi, Victoria 4, 13-21, 23, 24,
    30, 32, 37, 43, 51, 69, 111
    145, 157, 171, 191, 195,
    243, 244
Knowles, John 211
Knowles, Nancy 211

Lalewicz, Georg von 14
Langa, Celia 166
Letelier, Alfonso 19
Lévy, Lazare 15
Liszt, Franz 14
Llorente, Teodoro 145-146
Lorengar, Pilar 7
Ludwig, Claus-Dieter 145

Machado, Antonio 121-122
" Malato está el hijo del rey, El
    rey que muncho madruga" 157
Medina, S. J. Polo de 58
Menuhin, Yehudi 6
Mesa, Juan Bautista de 82
Milán, Luis de 69
Mompou, Federico 121
Morales, Maria 166, 245
Musica para un Códice
    Salmantino 19

Nin-Culmell, Joaquín 17
Noël, Sophie 62

Orán, Maria 121
Otein, Angeles 58

Pavana real 6, 19, 69
Penagos, Isabel 19, 158
Per la flor Lliri Blau 6, 16
Peribáñez y el Comendador de
    Ocaña 72
Pintos, Carlos Rodriguez 60
Pozo, Marími del 19, 58, 171-172
Preludio al gallo mañanero 6,
    15
Puig-Oriol, Josep Carner I, 146
Pujol, Emilio 17
Pujol, Matilde 17

Querol, Leopoldo 5

Robles, Maria Esther 80
Rodrigo, Cecilia 13, 111, 112
Rodrigo, Joaquín
    Biography 1-11
    Bird song 32, 195
    List of solo vocal works 8-11
Rodrigo, Pati 191
Rostropovich, Mstislav 6
Rubin, Pilar 158
Rubin, Walter 158
Rubio, Consuelo 63

Santillana, Marqués de 91, 100
Sanz, Gaspar 19

Schermant, Jack 236
Segovia, Andrés 19
Segura, Alfredo G. 26
Seoane, Blanca María Martínez 166
Shadows and Light (video) 23
Shaw, Guillermo Fernández 65
Sopeña, Federico 18
Supervia, Conchita 54

Toldrá, Eduardo, 231
"Triste estaba el rey David" 157

Vasquez, Juan 166

Vega, Lope de 47, 48, 71
Ventos, Josep Masso I 146
Veñas, Aurelio 47
Verdaguer, Jacinto 231-232
Verlasco, Angelina 19
Vicente, Gil 91-92
Villa-Lobos, Hector 19
Villancicos y canciones de navidad 51
Viñes, Ricardo 17

Walleghem, Alice van 32

Zarabanda Lejana y Villancico 5

Song Index

Aranjuez, ma pensée 24
En Aranjuez con tu amor 26
Barcarola 30
Canción del cucu 17, 32
Canción del grumete 5, 34
Canciones de dos épocas 91-109
    Cantiga 91
    Romance de la infantina de
        Francia 94
    Serranilla 100
    Árbol 105
    ¿Por qué te llamaré? 107
Canticel 35
Cántico de la esposa 16, 37
Cantos de amor y de guerra 111-119
    Paseábase el rey moro 112
    ¡A las armas, moriscotes! 113
    ¡Ay, luna que reluces! 114
    Sobre Baza estaba el rey 115
    Pastoricico, tú que has vuelto 118
La Chanson de ma vie 40
Chimères 40, 43
Con Antonio Machado 121-144
    Preludio 122

Mi corazón te aguarda 123
Tu voz y tu mano 126
Mañana de abril 128
Los sueños 131
Cantaban los niños 132
¿Recuerdas? 135
Fiesta en el prado 137
Abril galán 139
Canción del Duero 141
Coplas del pastor enamorado 16, 47, 83
Cuatre cançons en llengua catalana 35, 146-156
    Cançó del Teuladí 146
    Canticel 34, 35, 150
    L'Inquietut Primaveral de la Donzella 152
    Brollador Gentil 153
Cuatro canciones sefardies 157-163
    I. Respóndemos 158
    II. Una pastora yo ami 159
    III. Nani, nani 160
    IV. "Morena" me llaman 161

Cuatro madrigales amatorios 5,
    7, 18, 30, 165-170
  ¿Con qué la lavaré? 166
  Vos me matásteis 167
  ¿De dónde venís, amore? 168
  De los álamos vengo, madre 169
Doce canciones españolas 171-
    190
  1. ¡Viva la novia y el novio!
      172
  2. De ronda 173
  3. Una Palomita blanca 174
  4. Canción de baile con
      pandero 175
  5. Porque toco el pandero 177
  6. Tararán 178
  7. En las montañas de Asturias
      181
  8. Estando yo en mi majada 183
  9. Adela 184
  10. En Jerez de la Frontera 185
  11. San José y Maria 187
  12. Canción de cuna 1788
Dos canciones para cantar a los
  niños 191-194
  Corderito blanco 191
  Quedito 193
Dos poemas 195-203
  Verde verderol 196
  Pajaro del agua 199
La espera 50, 244
Esta Niña se lleva la flor 54

Estribillo 58
Fino cristal 60
Folias Canarias 62
La grotte 195, 205-210
Líricas castellanas 211-216
  San Juan y Pascua 212
  Despedida y soledad 213
  Espera del amada 215
Por mayo, era por mayo 63
  (Romancillo)
Primavera 65
Romance de Comendador de Ocana
    71
Romance de Durandarte 69
Rosaliana 85, 217-229
  1. Cantart'ei, Galicia 218
  2. ¿Por qué? 220
  3. Adiós ríos, adiós fontes 223
  4. ¡Vamos bebendo! 226
Sobre el cupey 80
Soneto 82
Triptico de Mosén Cinto 16, 231-
    242
  L'harpa sagrada 232
  Lo violí de Sant Francesch 236
  Sant Francesch y la cigala 239
¡Un Home, San Antonio! 84-88
Villancicos 7, 18, 50, 243-252
  Pastorcito santo 51, 244
  Aire y donaire 51, 248
  Coplillas de Belén 51, 250

About the Author

     Dr. Suzanne R. Draayer, soprano, is professor of music at Winona State University in Winona, Minnesota, where she teaches voice and related studies. Her teaching experience includes positions at Southern Utah University in Cedar City, Utah, Mary Washington College in Fredericksburg, Virginia, and the College of Charleston in Charleston, South Carolina. Dr. Draayer holds the Doctor of Musical Arts Degree in vocal performance, pedagogy, and literature from the University of Maryland. Her principal teachers there were James McDonald and George Shirley. She holds a Master of Science from Peabody College of Vanderbilt University (Nashville, Tennessee) and a Bachelor of Music from Furman University (Greenville, South Carolina).

     Dr. Draayer performs frequently in opera, oratorio, and recital. She has performed two seasons with the Maryland Handel Festival and several seasons for the Piccolo Spoleto Musica da Camera series and the Contemporary Women's series in Charleston, South Carolina. In January 1992, she performed on the Assembly Hall Concert Series at Temple Square in Salt Lake City. She has also presented concerts and lecture recitals for regional conferences of the College Music Society, the Utah Academy of Science, Arts and Letters, and for the National Association of Teachers of Singing. Recent engagements included recitals in Maryland, appearances with the La Crosse Symphony (La Crosse, Wisconsin) in November 1995,

and the 3M Orchestra (Minneapolis, Minnesota) in April 1996.
An avid advocator of Spanish music, Dr. Draayer frequently performs Spanish vocal literature has written extensively on the subject. Her article, *The Songs of Joaquín Turina--Tres Arias, Tres Poemas, and Tres Sonetas* was published in the September/October, 1993 issue of the **Journal of the National Association of Teachers of Singing.** A subsequent article, *Joaquín Rodrigo and his Doce Canciones Españolas and Cantos de amor y de guerra* was published in the March/April, 1995 issue of the **NATS Journal. A Singer's Guide to the Songs of Joaquín Rodrigo** was written after extensive interviews with the Rodrigo family. She has studied Spanish and Ladino diction with Nico Castel, multilinguist and diction coach at the Metropolitan Opera, the Julliard School, the Manhattan School of Music and Mannes College.

Dr. Draayer and the Winona State University Music Department are enthusiastically preparing for an international celebration of the works of Joaquín Rodrigo. The week-long festival of concerts, lectures, recitals, and special events is scheduled for November 2001, the one-hundredth birthday of the esteemed composer.